H. E. Smith,
Duxbury.
July 1902-

How to Make Baskets

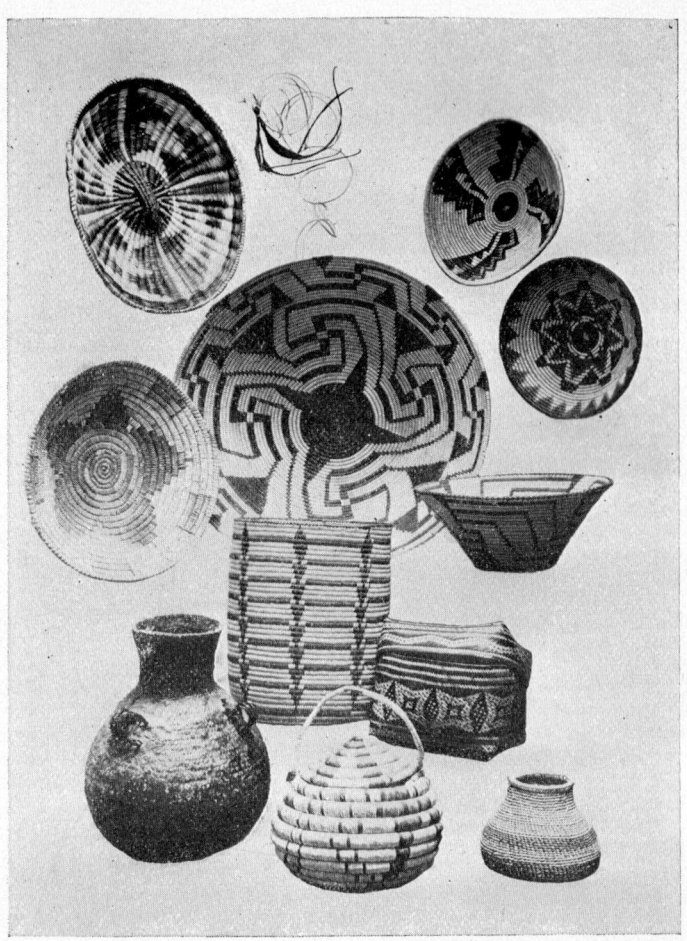

GRAIN PLAQUES—Of the Hopi, Apache, Havasupai and Pima Indians, from New Mexico and Arizona. PIMA SCRAP BASKET—Arrow-head design, avowedly adapted to white men's needs. RARE DOUBLE-WEAVE CHOCTAW COVERED BASKET—From Louisiana. PAIUTE GUMMED WICKER WATER-JAR—The handles of braided horse-hair. HOPI COILED YUCCA TREASURE BASKET—At the top of plate are strips of sisal willow and the seed vessel of the *Martynia* or "Cat Claws," from which most of the water-tight baskets in the Southwest are made.

TO
A. D. T.

PREFACE

THE twisting and weaving of Nature's materials, grasses, twigs, rushes and vines into useful and beautiful forms seems almost instinctive in man. Perhaps it came to him as the nest-weaving instinct comes to birds—for at first he used it as they do, in the building of his house. Later shields and boats were formed of wicker work but how long ago the first basket was made no one is wise enough to tell us. Today Indian tribes in South America weave baskets from their native palms, South African negroes use reeds and roots, while the Chinese and Japanese are wonderful workmen in this as in other arts and industries; but basketry has come down to us more directly through the American Indian. Generations of these weavers have produced masterpieces, many of which are preserved in our museums, and the young basket maker need not go on long pilgrimages to study the old masters of his craft. Here at last, as in England, the value of manual training is being realized, and basketry is taking an important place;

following the kindergarten and enabling the child to apply the principles he has learned there. He still works from the centre out and weaves as he wove his paper mats, but permanent materials have replaced the perishable ones and what he makes has an actual value.

Basketry also fills the need for a practical home industry for children; so not only in school, club and settlement but on home piazzas in summer, young weavers are taking their first lessons. Though they are unlearned in woodcraft, and have not the magic of the Indian squaw in their finger-tips, they can, and do, feel the fascination of basketry in the use of rattan, rush and raffia. It is hoped that this book may be a help in teaching them "How to Make Baskets."

CONTENTS

Preface v

CHAPTER I
Materials, Tools, Preparation, Weaving . 3

CHAPTER II
Raffia and Some of Its Uses . . 11

CHAPTER III
Mats and Their Borders . . . 21

CHAPTER IV
The Simplest Baskets 27

CHAPTER V
Covers 33

CHAPTER VI
Handles 51

CHAPTER VII
Work Baskets 65

CHAPTER VIII
Candy Baskets 83

CHAPTER IX
Scrap Baskets 101

CHAPTER X
Birds' Nests 113

CHAPTER XI
Oval Baskets 127

CHAPTER XII
The Finishing Touch . . . 149

CHAPTER XIII
How to Cane Chairs . . . 159

CHAPTER XIV
Some Indian Stitches . . . 169

CHAPTER XV
What the Basket Means to the Indian 181

LIST OF ILLUSTRATIONS

Frontispiece
>Grain Plaques, Pima Scrap Basket, Rare Double-Weave Choctaw Covered Basket, Paiute Gummed Wicker Water-Jar, Hopi Coiled Yucca Treasure Basket

Facing Page

Raffia and Some of its Uses	14
Mats and their Borders and the Simplest Baskets	22
Weaving a Small Basket	28
Covered Baskets	38
Large Mat and Dolls' Furniture	44
Basket with Handles	54
Some Work Baskets	70
Candy Baskets	92
Birds' Nests	116
Oval Baskets	136
Caning in a Frame and on a Chair	162
Twined Baskets	172
Coiled Baskets	176
Wicker Scoop, Basket Bowls, a Bottomless Bowl, Dinner Plates	182
Klikitat and Quinaielt Carrying Baskets	184
Alaskan Wallets, Carrying Baskets, Treasure Baskets, Plates and Aleutian Embroidered Wallet	186
Apache Grain Plaques and Jars	190
Rare Poma Ceremonial Basket, Mono Jar, Alaskan Treasure Basket, two Alaskan Carrying Baskets, a Squaw Cap, Cooking Basket	192

LIST OF FIGURES

		Page
Fig. 1	Twist of Rattan	4
" 2	Under-and-Over Weaving	5
" 3	Double Weaving	5
" 4	Pairing	6
" 5	Triple Twist	7
" 6		13
" 7		14
" 8		14
" 9		22
" 10		22
" 11	Joining Weavers	24
" 12		39
" 13		61
" 14		61
" 15		71
" 16		72
" 17		76
" 18		77
" 19	Napkin Ring	78
" 20		96
" 21		97
" 22		98
" 23		115
" 24		129
" 25		132
" 26		132
" 27		135
" 28		140

" 29 141
" 30 142
" 31 161
" 32 162
" 33 164
" 34 165
" 35 170
" 36 170
" 37 171
" 38 171
" 39 172
" 40 172
" 41 173
" 42 174
" 43 176
" 44 176
" 45 177
" 46 177
" 47 178

Materials, Tools, Preparation, Weaving

HOW TO MAKE BASKETS

CHAPTER I

MATERIALS, TOOLS, PREPARATION, WEAVING

Materials.—We shall use a great deal of rattan in making these baskets. It is a kind of palm which grows in the forests of India, twining about the trees and hanging in graceful festoons from the branches, sometimes to the length of five hundred feet, it is said, though seldom over an inch in diameter. It comes to us stripped of leaves and bark, and split into round or flat strips of various sizes, which are numbered by the manufacturer from 1 up to about 15, No. 1 being the finest as well as the most costly. Rattan can be bought (usually in five-pound lots) at basket factories in our large cities. Numbers 2, 3 and 4 are the best sizes for small baskets and 3, 5, and 6 for scrap baskets. Raffia, which is woven into small baskets, dolls' hats, etc., comes from Madagascar. It is a pale yellow material, soft and pliable, the outer cuticle of a palm, and can be bought at seed stores in hanks of about a pound each. Either braided and used by itself or woven flat on rattan spokes, it is easily handled by very young children, whose fingers are not strong enough to manage rattan.

The flat or braided rush which is imported by wholesale basket dealers comes in natural colors, dull green and soft wood-brown. The flat rush is sold by the pound, and the braided in bunches of ten metres each. Woven on rattan spokes, it makes beautiful baskets. Braided rush is a good material for scrap baskets, while the flat, being

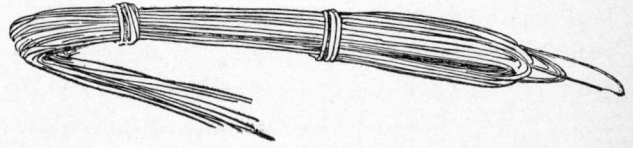

FIG. 1.—TWIST OF RATTAN

finer, is successfully woven into candy, flower and work baskets. The leaves of our own cat-tail furnish a material almost as pliable and quite as attractive in color as the imported rush; in fact, Nature's storehouse is full of possibilities to the weaver with a trained eye and hand.

Tools.—A pair of strong, sharp shears, a yardstick, and a deep paper pail for water are needed at first, and later a short steel knitting needle about the size of No. 4 rattan, and a sharp knife. Rubber finger guards for the right forefinger and thumb will be found almost a necessity where much weaving is done.

In raffia work, tapestry or worsted needles, No. 19, are required.

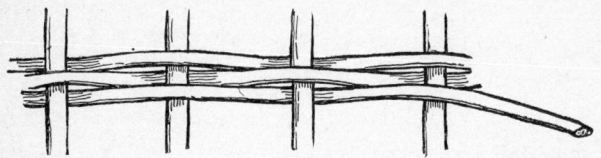

FIG. 2.—UNDER-AND-OVER WEAVING

Preparation.—The rattan, as it comes from the manufacturer, is in long twists or skeins. (See Fig. 1.) It should be drawn out, as it is needed, from the loop end; otherwise it will get tangled

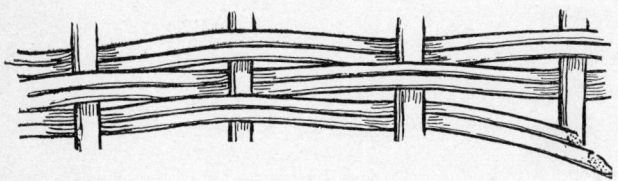

FIG. 3.—DOUBLE WEAVING

and broken. In preparing it, the spoke or heavy material which is to form the ribs of the basket (and which should be at least two numbers coarser than the weaver, except in small baskets, where a difference of one number is enough) is cut into lengths of the required number of inches. The weaver is wound into circles of about seven inches in diameter, the ends being twisted in and out several times to prevent unwinding. As rattan is very brittle, it should be put to soak, before using, for an hour in cold water, or fifteen minutes in hot Rush will not need to soak as long, and raffia will become pliable in a few seconds.

Weaving.—Under-and-over weaving, the simplest form of all, is the one most used.

Double weaving is done in the same way, except

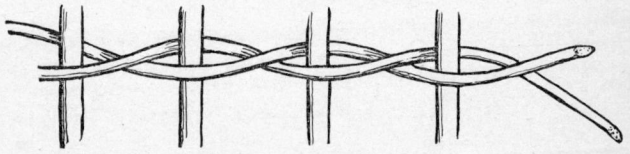

FIG. 4.—PAIRING

that two weavers are used at once. This is an effective weave on large surfaces, and in bands or patterns of the same or a contrasting color on plain rattan baskets.

Pairing may be used either with an odd or even number of spokes. Two weavers are started behind two succeeding spokes, and crossed between them, so that what was the under weaver becomes the upper one each time.

In the triple twist, three weavers are placed

behind three consecutive spokes and brought in succession, starting with the back one, over two and under one spoke, each on its way to the back of the third spoke being laid over the other two weavers. In turning up the sides of large baskets where separate spokes or additional spokes have

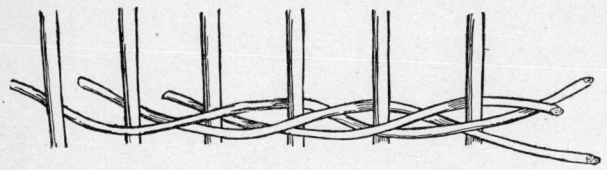

FIG. 5.—TRIPLE TWIST

been inserted, or as a strong top for scrap baskets, this weave is invaluable. It entirely hides the spokes it crosses, and therefore is often used to cover places where broken spokes have been replaced.

Raffia and Some of It's Uses

CHAPTER II

RAFFIA AND SOME OF ITS USES

It is a rare thing to find a material at once so soft and so strong as raffia; and it could hardly be better fitted for the work of children's fingers if it was made for the purpose. With a pound or two of raffia (there is about as much as this in one of the hanks that can be bought at seed stores or of dealers in kindergarten supplies), a paper of tapestry needles, a pair of scissors, and several flat sticks about a yard long and half an inch wide, you are well equipped. Given in addition to these some children fresh from the kindergarten training of eye and hand, and you can accomplish wonders. Indeed, so many charming things can be made from one of the great, yellow coils of raffia that it reminds one of the fairy tale in which the little gnome spun a roomful of straw into gold for the miller's daughter.

First of all, the children may braid some raffia, —we will use so much of it in this form, and now, as later in rattan work, it is well for them to learn to prepare the materials they are to work with. Three single strands of raffia may be used in braiding, if the plait is to be very fine; two pieces of the raffia in each strand makes a better size for general use. If the raffia is slightly dampened before the braiding is begun, it will work more smoothly. The ends are tied together and attached to a hook or chair back, and then the child braids to the end of the strands or until they become thin and spindling, when other strands are laid in, always on the under side, so that the little ends will not show on the upper or right side. These ends may be cut quite close when the braid is done. It is hardly necessary to say that the braiding should be even and firm.

Knotted Work Bag

Materials: 24 strands of raffia,
A stick about a yard long and 1½ inches wide,
A pair of scissors,
A tapestry needle.

The stick is held by the left hand at right angles with the body, the end resting on a chair or table. A strand of raffia is doubled and tied around the stick, as shown in Fig. 6, the knot being drawn up quite close. Twenty-four strands are knotted on in this way; they are then placed about an inch apart, and beginning with the inner one of the two strands nearest the workman, it is knotted, at about an inch from the first row of knots, with the strand nearest it in the next pair, making an even mesh. This is continued across the stick, and another row is knotted and another until ten or twelve rows have been made, when the work will tend toward a V shape (see Fig. 7, which for convenience is drawn with fewer strands). The stick is now slipped out and the bag finished (see Fig 8) by knotting first the two loose strands at the top together, then the two pairs following, and so on until the bottom is reached. The two sides are joined at the bottom by placing them with the meshes and knots evenly together and knotting two strands from the front and two from the back together each time in a last row of knotting. The ends of the raffia when cut to an even length make a fairly satisfactory finish, but the following is a better one: Wind a strand of raffia over a card, about two and a quarter inches wide, five or six

FIG. 6

times, then slip it off and bind it around several times near the top with the end of the strand, sewing it fast with a tapestry needle; this forms a little tassel, such as are made of worsted. A row of these across the bottom of the bag, a cord of

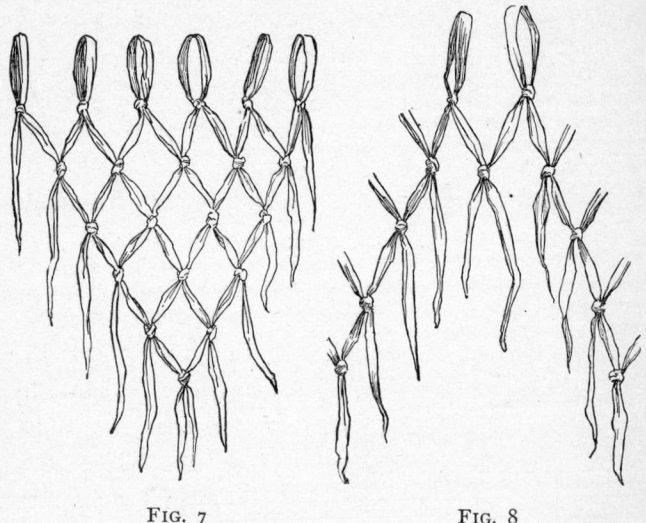

FIG. 7 FIG. 8

twisted raffia (as worsted cords are made), drawn through the top loops and an inner lining of turkey-red cotton will complete this pretty and serviceable bag

RAFFIA AND SOME OF ITS USES

Knotted Bag for Twine

Materials: 17 strands of raffia,
A stick the size of a lead pencil,
A pair of scissors,
A ball of twine,
A tapestry needle.

It will be well to get your ball of twine before beginning this bag, to make sure of its fitting. A common lead pencil, provided it is a long one, will do quite as well as a special stick, and the raffia is knotted on it as described in the directions for a work bag, only there are seventeen strands instead of twenty-four; they are placed closer together, not over a quarter of an inch apart, and the rows of knotting are about a quarter of an inch from each other. When twelve rows are completed, the work is slipped off and finished as in the work bag. The bottom should be drawn up tightly, with a needleful of raffia, and a ball of twine of some bright harmonious color slipped in. . A cord to gather up the loops at the top and a large tassel at the bottom will be the finishing touches to a dainty gift that any child may be proud to offer as his own work

Book-Mark

Materials: 1 spoke 10 inches long of No. 6 flat rattan,
3 spokes 3¼ inches long of No. 6 flat rattan,
1 strand of raffia,
A tapestry needle.

A book-mark that is pretty and easily woven is made on an Indian pattern, with the Indian arrangement of spokes and weavers. After soaking the spokes for an hour in cold water, the long spoke, No. 1, is laid on a table vertically; No. 2, one of the short spokes, is then placed across it horizontally, at a distance of a little over an inch and a half from the end. Number 3, a short spoke, is laid across the other two obliquely, to the right of the upper end of spoke No. 1, and between it and the right end of spoke No. 2. Number 4 crosses from the left of spoke No. 1 obliquely, completing the star shape. A strand of raffia is doubled at its centre around spoke No. 1, with the ends toward the right. It is woven by pairing (see Chapter I) to a distance of one inch from the tip of each spoke, when the ends of the raffia are threaded through a worsted or tapestry needle and sewed off under the weaving, and the tips of the short spokes are cut in points.

Raffia Mat

Materials: 6 yards of braided raffia,
Several strands of loose raffia,
A tapestry needle,
A pair of scissors.

The braided raffia previously prepared now comes into use. A tapestry needle is threaded with a fine strand of raffia, and the mat is begun by winding the end of the braid several times with the end of the strand which is threaded through the needle. A coil is then started with the end of the braid, the edge of the braid being up, not the face, and it is sewed through at least three braids at a time in stitches which run in the direction of the twists in the braid. The needle is run in slanting down from right to left and then up from right to left, forming a V within the coil. The mat is coiled round and round in this way till it is about four inches in diameter, when a border of the braid, sewed on in loops, completes it. These mats may be dyed or stained, or a large, colored bead is sometimes sewed in each loop of the border.

Doll's Hat

Materials: 2 yards of braided raffia,
A tapestry needle,
Several strands of loose raffia,
A pair of scissors.

The idea of making her own doll's hats will be a delightful and novel one to the small girl, and hats of all sizes and shapes are possible when she has once mastered the sewing together of the braided raffia. Just as in large hats we will start with the very centre of the crown, and that is coiled and sewed in the same way as the raffia mat was done, till it is an oval mat about one and a half by two inches; the coil of braid is then brought round with its upper edge just below the centre of the previous row. The next row is sewed around in the same way and the next until the crown is the desired height. We shall have to be careful to draw the braid tight, and in sewing to make the stitches run like the twists in the braid so that they will show as little as possible. The brim is made by flattening out the braid and letting it go more easily, taking care, however, to see that it overlaps the last row nearly to the centre of the braid in each case. When the brim is about an inch wide, one or two rows are drawn quite tightly as they are sewed on, which gives a roll to the edge of the brim, and it is finished by sewing the end of the braid firmly down on the under side of the brim. Many soft raffia baskets, oval and round, can be made on the principle of the crown of this hat, and we shall learn in subsequent chapters how to make more elaborate baskets of this material.

Mats and Their Borders

CHAPTER III

MATS AND THEIR BORDERS

THE centre, which forms the bottom of the basket is the starting-point, and it is such an important part to master that we will make at least two centres in the form of mats before beginning a basket.

Mat with Open Border No. 1

Materials: 4 12-inch spokes of No. 4 rattan,
1 7-inch spoke of No 4 rattan,
1 weaver of No. 2 rattan.

The four spokes, arranged in pairs, are crossed in the centre, the vertical ones being uppermost or nearest the person weaving; and between the upper halves of these vertical spokes the half spoke seven inches long is placed. These are held in position by the left hand, which is, as always, the one that holds while the right is the weaving hand. An end of the weaver previously unwound is placed along the horizontal spoke back of the vertical ones with the end toward the right. The forefinger of the right hand now presses the weaver across the upper vertical spokes and down behind the horizontal ones on the right (thus binding the end of the weaver securely), next over the lower vertical spokes, and behind the horizontal ones on the left (see Fig. 9). This is repeated, and then beginning with the upper vertical spokes, the spokes are separated and the weaving begins (see Fig. 10). A common fault of beginners is to pull the weaver from a distance of several inches from the work; instead it should be

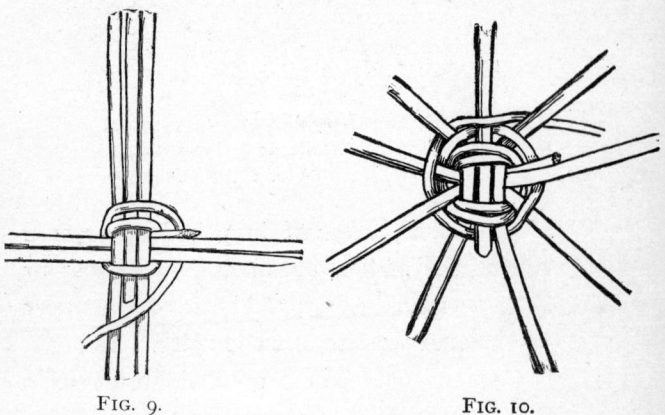

FIG. 9. FIG. 10.

pressed with the forefinger, under and over the spokes, as close to the work as it is possible to get it. The spokes should be very evenly separated— this is something that the beginner cannot be too careful about, as upon it so much of the symmetry and strength of his baskets will depend. It may

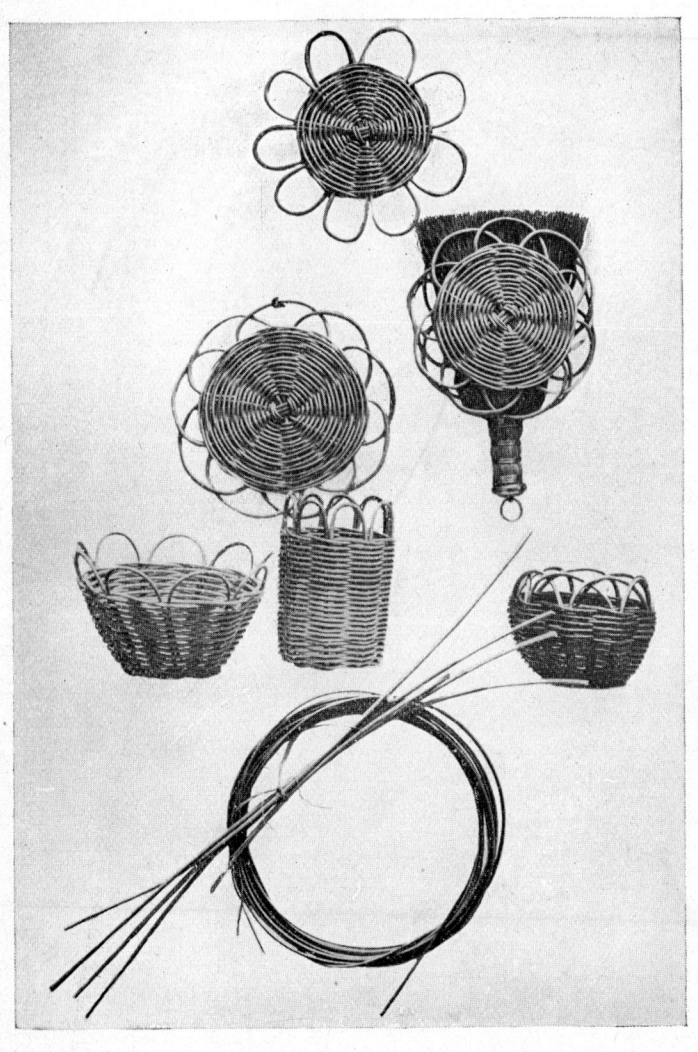

MATS AND THEIR BORDERS AND THE SIMPLEST BASKETS

help him to think of the regular spaces between the spokes of a wheel and how much trouble one badly placed spoke would make. When there is just enough weaver left to go around once, the binding off is begun. This is a process much like overcasting. After going under one spoke and over another, the weaver is passed under the last row of weaving just before it reaches the next spoke, it then goes behind that spoke, in front of the next and under the last row of weaving before the next spoke. When a row of this binding is completed, the mat is finished with

Open Border No. 1.—After cutting the spokes to a uniform length with a slanting cut (so that the point may be easily pushed down between the weavers), the spokes should be held in water for a few minutes. When quite pliable, spoke No. 1 is pushed down beside spoke No. 2, No. 2 beside No. 3, and so on around the mat, taking care that at least an inch is pressed below the edge of the mat.

Mat with Two Weavers and Open Border No. 2

> **Materials:** 4 14-inch spokes of No. 4 rattan,
> 1 8-inch spoke of No. 4 rattan,
> 2 weavers of No. 2 rattan.

This mat is started like the first one and woven in the same way until the end of the first weaver is reached, when another is joined to it by simply crossing the weavers, at an inch from the end of each, back of a spoke (See Fig. 11). The ends may need to be held, or replaced in position while

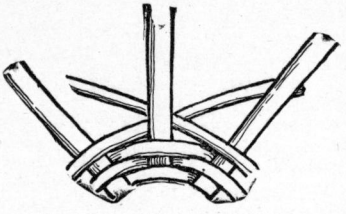

FIG. 11.—Joining Weavers.

weaving one row after which they will keep their places and may be cut shorter when the mat or basket is finished and dry. This method of joining weavers has the advantage of not showing on the right side of the work. When the end of the second weaver is reached, bind off as in the first mat and finish with

Open Border No. 2.—Spokes at least four inches long, measuring from the last row of weaving, are required for this border. Cut and soak as described in Open Border No. 1. Spoke No. 1 crosses No. 2 and is pushed down beside No. 3. Number 2 crosses No. 3 and is pushed down beside No. 4 and so on around the mat.

Even these first little mats are useful to put under a tea-pot on the table, or two tied together with ribbons or with their borders interlaced will make a serviceable whisk-broom holder.

The Simplest Baskets

CHAPTER IV

THE SIMPLEST BASKETS

IN weaving the first baskets, while the worker is getting familiar with his material, he should copy such simple forms as are shown in the plate. The working out of his own ideas will follow later.

Basket with Open Border No. 1

Materials: 4 14-inch spokes of No. 3 rattan,
1 8-inch spoke of No. 3 rattan,
2 weavers of No 2 rattan.

Begin as in the directions for a mat, and when the centre or bottom of the basket is about two inches in diameter, wet the spokes and bend them sharply upward, remembering always that the side toward the person weaving is the outside of the basket, and that the weaving should go from left to right. This is something that even skillful young workmen sometimes need to have impressed upon them. The bottom of the basket should be placed on the knee with the side which in starting was toward the worker turned down, the spokes bent upward, and the weaving done in that position. In weaving up the sides of the basket, the middle finger of the right hand presses down each spoke behind which the weaver has to go, while the thumb and forefinger bring the weaver along behind it. Two weavers are used, and they are joined by simply crossing them, at an inch from the end of each, behind a spoke. After binding off, finish with Open Border No. 1.

Basket with Rounding sides and Open Border No. 2

Materials: 4 14-inch spokes of No. 3 rattan,
1 8-inch spoke of No. 3 rattan,
2 weavers of No. 2 rattan.

Having made a bottom about two inches in diameter, wet the spokes and turn them up, rounding them by bending them over the middle finger. The first weaver should not be drawn too tight, but allowed to go easily, though pressed closely down upon the weaving just below it. Before the middle of the second weaver is reached the spokes should be gradually drawn closer together by a slight tightening of the weaver; this should continue to the end of the weaver. Bind off and finish with Open Border No. 2. This is an important basket in teaching the effect of a loosely and a tightly drawn weaver. Both this basket and the one with

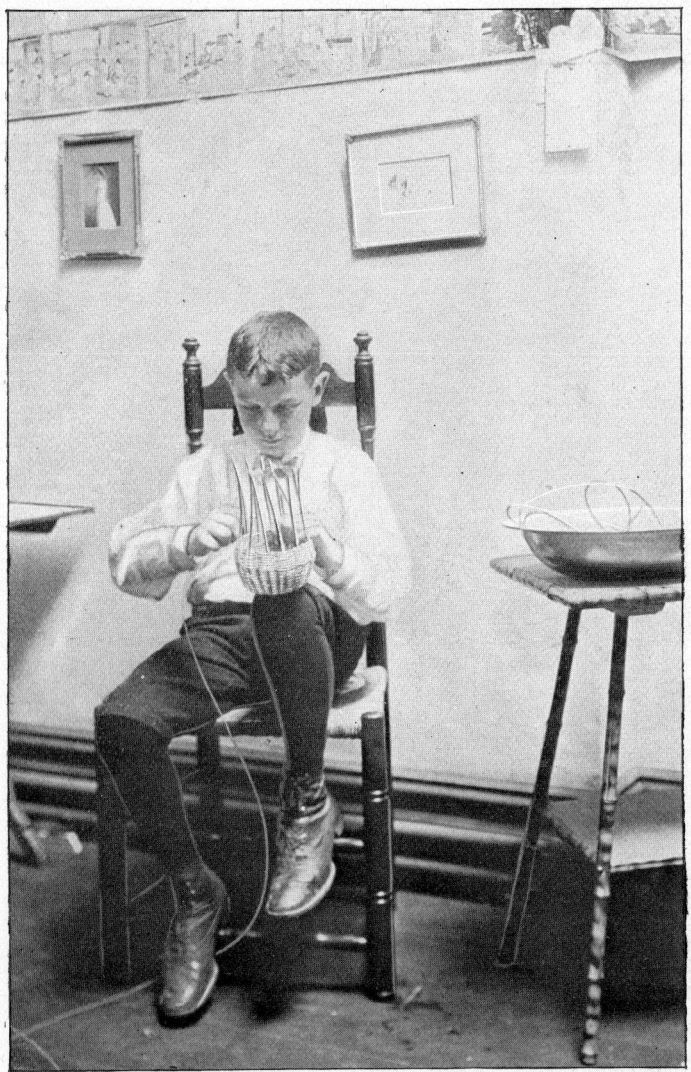
WEAVING A SMALL BASKET
This illustrates the way in which small baskets are held while weaving the sides

straight sides make pretty candy baskets, especially when they are dyed or stained attractively; see Chapter XII.

Stand for Pens and Pencils with Open Border No. 1

Materials: 4 14-inch spokes of No. 4 rattan,
1 8-inch spoke of No. 4 rattan,
2½ weavers of No. 2 rattan.

Any child who has successfully made the mats and baskets already described will be able to form this stand and it will interest him to see how useful it will be on someone's desk.

After weaving a centre almost two and a quarter inches in diameter, the spokes are turned sharply upward, and the weaving of the sides is begun; this will be a little harder than the weaving of the first two baskets because the sides should be kept perfectly straight all the way up. To do this there must be an even pressure on the weaver, neither too tight nor too loose, and the spokes must be kept the same distance apart from the bottom to the top. The spoke material being heavier than in the other baskets helps to keep the sides firm. Two weavers and part of a third are used; the edge is then bound off and Open Border No. 1 finishes it.

Covers

CHAPTER V

COVERS

In weaving larger baskets the number of spokes as well as their length must of course be increased and in order to accustom himself to the handling of these extra spokes the worker is advised to make a

Large Mat with Open Border No. 2

Materials: 6 16-inch spokes of No. 4 rattan,
1 9-inch spoke of No. 4 rattan,
3 weavers of No. 2 rattan.

Three vertical and three horizontal spokes are arranged as in the first mat, and the half spoke (so called for convenience but which is, as always, one inch longer than half the length of the others, to allow for binding) is placed between any two of the upper vertical spokes. It should never be on the outside of the group. A weaver is started and bound around three times, the spokes are then separated and the weaving begins. Three weavers are used and then the mat is bound off and finished with Open Border No. 2.

The child who does not appreciate mats will be entirely won over when he sees some of the fascinating things that can be made with them. For example a tiny wicker table just the size for a doll's house and the shape for an afternoon tea!

Doll's Table of Rattan

Materials: 6 22-inch spokes of No. 3 rattan,
1 12-inch spoke of No. 3 rattan,
1 weaver of No. 2 rattan,
A piece of fine wire 2 or 3 inches long,
Raffia,
A knitting needle.

Two groups of spokes, one of three and the other of three and a half, are crossed in the centre and woven into a mat, which when it is three and a half inches in diameter is bound off. Each spoke is brought across the next one and pressed down beside the next as in Open Border No. 2, with the difference that the long end is not cut off, but brought out between the fourth and fifth rows of weaving on the under side of the mat. The border is drawn in so that it will not be over a quarter of an inch beyond the weaving. The long ends of the spokes (which are to form the legs of the table) are brought together and bound with a piece of fine wire just under the centre. They are then separated into three groups of four each. The odd spoke is either cut off or whittled very thin and bound in with one of the three groups. A strand of raffia, either double or single, is now started at the top of one of the groups and wound tightly around until it has covered the desired length. At the end a half hitch, or one button-hole stitch, is made to keep the raffia from slipping and then it is wound up again to the top. It is brought down the second leg as far as the first one was wound, then it is turned with a half hitch and brought up again in the same way. The third leg is also wound down and up again with a half hitch at the bottom to hold it. After this third leg has been covered the raffia is brought in and out between the legs where they separate in order to spread them more effectually. It is then tied and the ends cut close. Finally the spokes at the end of each leg are cut to a uniform length, and slanting, so that the table will stand firmly.

Doll's Chair of Rattan

Materials: 6 20-inch spokes of No. 3 rattan
1 11-inch spoke of No. 3 rattan,
4 10-inch spokes of No. 3 rattan,
1 piece of No. 3 rattan about 9 inches long,
2 weavers of No. 2 rattan,
Raffia
A knitting needle

Again the mat comes into play. This time as the seat of a miniature high backed chair made of rattan. Groups of twenty-inch spokes, one of three and the other of three and a half, are crossed in the centre, bound around twice with a weaver of No. 2 rattan and woven into a mat three inches in diameter. Each spoke is brought down beside the next one, as in Open Border No. 1, except that the long end is threaded through between the second and third rows of weaving on the under side of the mat. When all have been brought out in this way underneath the mat, or seat, the four groups of three ends each which are to form the legs, should be so divided that the vertical spokes in the centre of the chair seat shall run toward the front and back of the seat. The thirteenth spoke is whittled to a thin point and bound in with one of the other groups, which are wound with raffia down to the end, turned with a half hitch and then brought up again. A neat way to start the raffia is to thread it across a row of weaving just above the group it is to bind. A ring of No. 3 rattan about nine inches long is coiled and held within the space inclosed by the legs, about half way down, where it is wound around with a strand of raffia and bound securely to each leg The back of the chair is formed by inserting a number of spokes of No. 3

rattan, ten inches long beside those in the seat and at that part of the seat which has been chosen for the back. It is woven back and forth with No. 2 weaver. Needless to say the weaver must be a very pliable one in order to make the sharp turns that are necessary on the sides. Individual taste and skill here has an excellent opportunity to show itself, and an ingenious child will find that he can construct almost any kind of a back he chooses. The outside spokes of the chair back in the picture are each brought over and down beside the other one; while the inner spokes are crossed in the centre and run down beside the outer spokes, forming a narrow, oval back which is woven back and forth as far up as the crossing of the inner spokes. If arms are desired more spokes will be necessary. In this case the outer spokes are woven in with the others for a few rows and then bent over and forward to form the arms. They are cut to the desired length and each is inserted beside one of the side spokes in the seat. Having exhausted, for the present, the possibilities of the mat we will return to the real subject of the chapter—covers, with apologies for the digression.

Small Round Basket with Slightly Rounded Cover

Materials: BASKET—6 16-inch spokes of No. 4 rattan,
1 9-inch spoke of No. 4 rattan,
4 weavers of No. 2 rattan.
COVER, HINGE, ETC.—6 14-inch spokes of No. 4 rattan,
1 8-inch spoke of No 4 rattan,
1½ weavers of No. 2 rattan,
A knitting needle.

The bottom is woven in the same way as the large mat, to a diameter of one and three-eighths inches; when the spokes are wet and rounded up over the finger. The sides are woven with loosely drawn weavers until three have been used. The fourth weaver is drawn tighter so that the basket shall be somewhat the shape of an orange with the top cut off. The edge is bound and finished with this border. The spokes are soaked until pliable, and each is brought back of the next one on the right and then out. This goes on around the basket. The end of each spoke in turn is then brought over the first spoke on the right, and pressed down inside the basket just behind the second spoke on the right and next to the weaving.

The cover is woven like the bottom, except that from the very centre the spokes are bent gradually up. One full-length weaver should make a large enough cover. It is then bound off and finished with a Rope Border. Each spoke in succession is

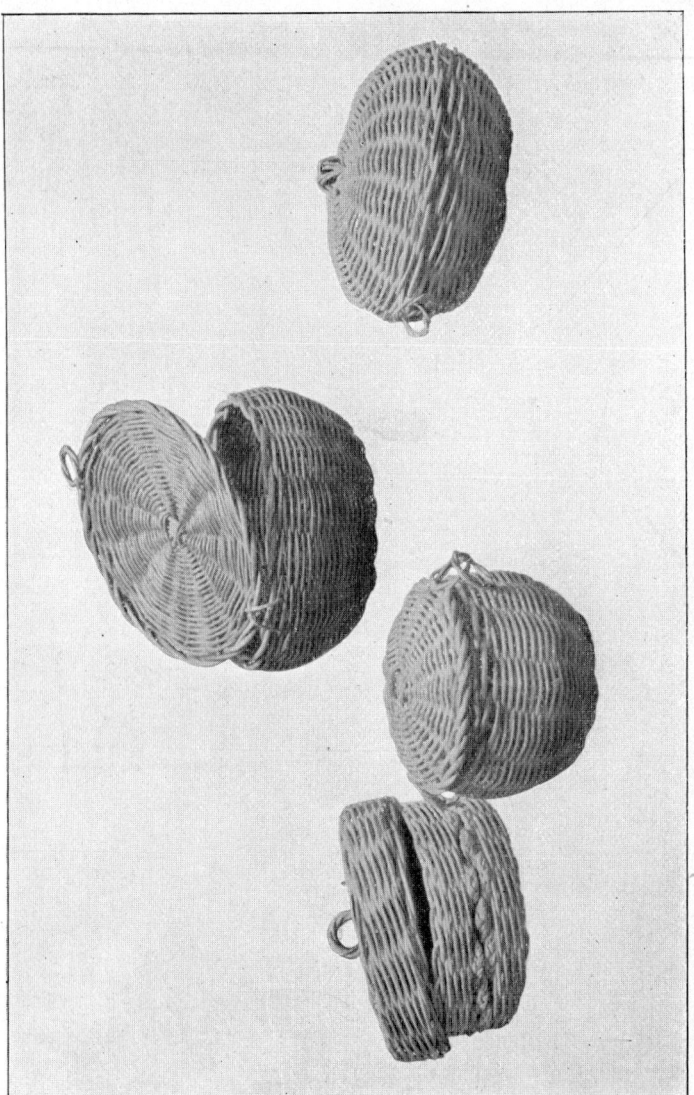

COVERED BASKETS

The small rattan basket with a slightly rounded cover, which is shown in the foreground, is the simplest of these baskets. The cover of the one on the right is as deep as the basket itself. Above and to the left is a pale green basket with a flat cover, and the one on the extreme left has a band of braided raffia on basket and cover

brought across the next spoke to the right and then inside the cover. When the circuit of the cover has been made, each end of a spoke is brought across the next spoke to the right and then pressed down inside the cover where, after the border is finished, they are cut just long enough to allow each end to lie across the next spoke.

Fastenings. Three rings of No. 2 rattan are made as follows. A piece of rattan about a foot long, which has been soaked until pliable, is tied into a ring. The ends are then twisted in and out once around the foundation ring (see Fig. 12), or when a heavier ring is required, twice or three times. One of the rings should be smaller than the other two, and none of them need be over three-quarters of an inch in diameter. The smallest one is attached to the cover in front, across a spoke and between the border and the last row of weaving, each end being sewed off under a spoke, then over one and inside the cover, where it is cut off. Another ring is attached in the same

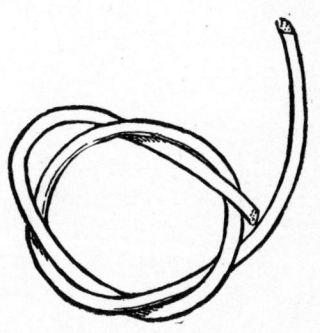

FIG. 12.

way at the back of the cover, and the third one is fastened across a spoke in the front of the basket, between the third and fourth rows of weaving. To complete the hinge the cover is put in position so that the ring at the back of the cover will be just above a spoke on the basket. The end of a small piece of No. 2 weaver is then pressed in between the third and fourth rows of weaving to the left of the spoke referred to, and brought out on the right of the spoke. The ends are then crossed, brought through the ring on the cover, and drawn up just tight enough to allow the cover to close easily. The end which started on the left of the spoke is brought to the right and fastened, as the rings were, between the border and the last row of weaving on the basket, while the end which started from the right of the spoke crosses to the left, and is fastened in the same way between the border and the last row of weaving. If desired this basket may be varnished, see Chapter XII.

Green Rattan Basket with Flat Cover

Materials: BASKET—8 16-inch spokes of No. 4 rattan,
1 9-inch spoke of No. 4 rattan,
5½ weavers of No. 2 rattan.
COVER, HINGE, ETC.—6 16-inch spokes of No. 4 rattan,
1 9-inch spoke of No. 4 rattan,
4 weavers of No. 2 rattan,
A knitting needle.

This is an excellent shape for candy or for a small work basket and though it is so simple if it is well made and colored the result is most satisfactory. The basket is started with eight sixteen and one nine-inch spoke of No. 4 rattan, bound three times with No. 2 weaver and woven into a bottom three inches and a quarter in diameter. The spokes are then wet and rounded up into a bowl shape which, when five weavers have been used in under-and-over weaving, should be drawn in gradually with the remaining half weaver until the top of the basket is five and a half inches in diameter. It is then bound off and finished with this border. Each spoke is brought over the next one on the right and pressed down inside the basket where, after the border is finished, the ends are cut just long enough to allow each to lie against the spoke in front of it.

The cover has two groups of sixteen-inch spokes, one of three and the other of three and a half which are crossed in the usual way and bound three times. It is woven like the large mat until its diameter is about five inches when the edge is bound off and finished with the Rope Border already described on page 39.

The hinge and fastening are made as follows. Having chosen the best place for the hinge on basket and cover an end of a piece of No. 2 rattan, about a foot long, (which has been wet until pliable) is inserted at the right of a spoke and under the last row of weaving on the basket. It is then woven under and over two or three spokes to fasten it securely. The long end is crossed diagonally over the border of the cover and pressed in between the last two rows of weaving at the left of a spoke. It is then brought down inside and out again at the left of the spoke on the basket and across to the right of the spoke in the cover, where it is pressed inside and down to the place where it started on the basket. Here it is woven under and over several spokes till it is firmly attached. The front fastening is formed of two rings, also made of No. 2 rattan, see page 39. The ring on the cover should be smaller than the one on the basket so that it may slip through it. In attaching the one on the cover, the ends are pushed inside the basket between the border and the last row of weaving, and woven under and over two or three spokes until the ring is secure. The ring on the basket is fastened in the same way, except that the ends are inserted between the fourth and fifth rows of weaving from the top, one on either side of a spoke. The basket is then colored pale green, see Chapter XII.

Basket with Deep Cover having Rounded Sides

Materials: BASKET—8 18-inch spokes of No. 3 rattan,
1 10-inch spoke of No. 3 rattan,
4 weavers of No. 2 rattan.
COVER AND FASTENINGS—8 18-inch spokes of No. 3 rattan,
1 10-inch spoke of No. 3 rattan,
5 weavers of No. 2 rattan,
A knitting needle.

A bottom, slightly raised in the centre, is woven to a diameter of two and a half inches. After the spokes have been wet until pliable they are bent up in a rounded flare, like a saucer in shape. Four weavers are used in under-and-over weaving, and the basket should then be about five and a quarter inches in diameter. The edge is bound off and a border made in this way. Each spoke is brought under the next spoke on the right, then over one and inside of the basket. The first part of the border should be left loose and open so that the last spokes can be more easily woven in.

The cover is made in the same way as the basket, except that the spokes are bent gradually up from the centre in a rounded flare. When four weavers have been used, and the cover is exactly the size of the basket, it is bound off and completed with the simple border made by bringing each spoke over the one on the right and down inside.

A ring (see Fig. 12) is attached to the front of

the cover, another one at the back, and a third and slightly larger one is fastened on to the basket (just below the one on the front of the cover) across a spoke, and between the second and third rows of weaving from the top.

A knob by which to lift the cover is made of a pliable piece of No. 2 rattan about a foot long. A knitting needle is run in between the spokes and the binding, at the right of the upper vertical spokes in the centre of the cover, making a space through which an end of the piece of rattan is inserted and fastened off on the wrong side, by weaving it under and over one or two spokes. The long end is brought diagonally across to the left of the lower vertical spokes, where it is pushed through (with the aid of the knitting needle) leaving a loop about half an inch high on top. It then crosses on the wrong side to the place where it started.

This is repeated until there are four loops of the same height and close together. The end is then brought out at the right of the lower vertical spokes and woven over the first two loops, under the next two, and in at the left of the upper vertical spokes. The second time across, it is again brought over the first two loops and under the second. The third time the weaver crosses, it goes under the first two loops, over the second and

LARGE MAT AND DOLL'S FURNITURE

The starting of a large mat is shown at the upper left-hand corner of the plate, with the finished mat beside it. The tiny chair, table and foot-stool are begun in the same way.

in; while the fourth follows the third in the same way. The end is then fastened off on the wrong side, completing the knob.

Basket with Overlapping Cover

Materials: BASKET—8 18-inch spokes of No. 3 rattan,
1 10-inch spoke of No. 3 rattan,
4½ weavers of No. 2 rattan,
6 strands of raffia, braided.
COVER AND RING—8 16-inch spokes of No. 3 rattan,
1 9-inch spoke of No. 3 rattan,
4 or 5 weavers of No. 2 rattan,
6 strands of raffia, braided,
A knitting needle.

Before beginning this basket the raffia will have to be braided, as described in Chapter II, into two pieces of equal length; one for the band on the basket and the other for the cover. The bottom of the basket is woven, slightly raised in the centre, to a diameter of four and a half inches; the spokes are then wet until pliable and turned sharply upward. Straight sides are woven of half an inch of triple twist, then three rows of braided raffia and another half inch of triple twist, which should end at the same place on the circumference of the basket as it began. In ending, each weaver is cut just long enough to allow it to be pressed down beside the next spoke for about half an inch below the edge of the basket. The border is woven from right to left (instead of left to right as is usual in closed borders), which makes it harmonize better with the triple twist. Each spoke is brought under the spoke to the left, over the next spoke and down inside; the beginning of the border being left open so that the last spokes may be easily woven in.

Cover.—Eight and a half sixteen-inch spokes are divided into two groups, one of four and the other of four and a half, and started in a flat centre which is woven to a diameter of an inch and three-quarters. The braided raffia is then joined to the rattan, by crossing the ends back of a spoke, and woven into four rows. The rattan is then started again and continued in under-and-over weaving until the cover is five inches in diameter when the spokes are thoroughly wet and turned sharply upward. Seven-eighths of an inch of triple twist is woven into straight sides for the overlapping cover. It is finished with a border in one row, woven from right to left as was the border of the basket. Each spoke is brought over the next spoke, under the succeeding one and then out, where it is cut, after the border is made, just long enough to allow the end to lie against the spoke in front.

A ring, not quite an inch in diameter, of No. 2 rattan twisted around three times, is a necessary addition. It makes a sturdy little handle with which to raise the cover. After the ends have been twisted around the circumference of the ring as described elsewhere in this chapter, they are inserted, with the aid of a knitting needle, one on either side of the vertical spokes in the very centre of the cover, and woven under and over one or two spokes till firmly fastened, when they are cut off on the inside.

Handles

CHAPTER VI

HANDLES

SUCH handles as are described in this chapter are simple and quite possible for the beginner to make. Others that are more elaborate will be found in the chapter on Oval Baskets.

Small Basket with Twisted Handle

Materials: BASKET—6 16-inch spokes of No. 4 rattan,
 1 9-inch spoke of No. 4 rattan,
 2 weavers of No. 2 rattan,
HANDLE—1 12-inch spoke of No. 4 rattan,
 1 weaver of No. 2 rattan,
 A knitting needle.

Six spokes and a half are started as in the large mat and woven into a centre, which should be pressed up in the middle into a concave form like the bottom of a wine bottle. Beginners often find it hard to make a basket that will stand well. The tendency seems to be to form a rounded bottom rather than one that is perfectly flat. A bottom that is slightly concave is not so difficult to make, and answers the purpose as well as a flat one. When the bottom is two inches in diameter the spokes are wet and bent upward and woven with flaring sides. Two weavers are used, and then the basket is bound off and finished with a closed border.

After wetting the spokes until they are pliable the border, which is in two rows, is begun. The first spoke is brought behind the spoke to the right of it and then out, leaving a space between the basket and the first spoke. The second spoke is brought behind the one to the right of it and then out in the same way, except that it is pressed close down upon the basket. Each spoke in turn is brought back and out until there is only one left erect. This spoke is brought behind the first spoke, out between the first and second spokes and pressed close down upon the weaving. In the second row each spoke is brought behind the succeeding one on the right and then out, making a roll on the edge of the basket with the ends outside. These ends are cut slanting, just long enough to allow each to rest on the spoke in front of it.

Handle.—The knitting needle is run down beside a spoke and then drawn out leaving room to insert an end of the twelve inch spoke, which should be pressed down at least an inch below the top of the basket. The other end of the spoke is then inserted in the same way beside a spoke exactly opposite where the first end was placed. This makes the foundation handle. The end of a pliable weaver is now inserted under the third row from the top of the basket to the left of the foundation handle and run up between the weaving. This weaver is twisted around the handle with twists about an inch and a half apart (experience will soon show that twists too near together will make an uneven handle and those too far apart one that is not firm and strong). At the opposite side of the basket the weaver is pushed in, under the third row of weaving from the top, on one side of the handle and brought out again on the other side of the handle three rows from the top, making a loop inside. The weaver is then laid close beside the first twist, and follows it across to the opposite side, where it goes in under the third row on the left of the handle and comes out on the right side. Each row of twisting must follow close beside the last and six, or at most seven, rows will cover the spoke. The weaver is fastened off by bringing it inside the basket, then out across a spoke and inside the basket again where it is cut short.

Basket with Small Side Handles

Materials: BASKET—8 24-inch spokes of No. 4 rattan,
 1 13-inch spoke of No. 4 rattan,
 4½ weavers of No. 2 rattan.
HANDLES—2 22-inch pieces of No. 4 rattan,
 A knitting needle.

Strong practical handles are in keeping with the plain bowl shaped basket in the picture, which is rather like a doll's clothes basket and may be used for one. After weaving a slightly concave bottom, four inches in diameter, the spokes are wet and bent upward; rounding them over the finger as described elsewhere. The sides are gradually flared until, when four full length weavers and a half have been used, the basket is seven and a quarter inches in diameter. The top is then bound off and completed with a border as follows. In the first row, each spoke is brought back of the next one on the right and then out. In the second row, each spoke is brought back of the succeeding one on the right and then out. The third row is made by bringing each end over the next spoke on the right, and pushing it inside the basket just back of the succeeding spoke and directly above the weaving.

Handles.—In making the handles the two twenty-two inch pieces of rattan are soaked until

BASKETS WITH HANDLES

The simplest handle is that on the small basket at the left of the foreground. Another simple handle is the braided one beside it. Below and to the right is a basket with small side handles. Above is the rattle with its handle of wound cane, and above that is shown the basket with large ring handles, and, most elaborate of all, the handle with interlaced ends

they are pliable. Then one is started in this way: After the knitting needle has been pushed down on the left of a spoke, to make way between the weavers, an end of the twenty-two inch piece of rattan is pressed down about three-quarters of an inch below the top of the weaving. The long end is brought across one spoke, not counting the one beside which it started, and down inside the basket at the left of the next spoke and just under the border; making the foundation handle which, at its widest part, should not be over an inch from the basket. The end is now brought out on the right of the spoke and twisted around the foundation handle. About three twists should bring it to the other side of the handle where it is pushed down inside the basket on the right of the spoke and out again on the left. It then twists around the handle across to the right side, where the end is cut off, leaving about an inch which is pressed down between the weavers to the right of the spoke. The second handle is made in the same way, taking care that it shall be so placed on the basket as to be exactly opposite the first one.

Flower Basket with High Braided Handle

Materials: BASKET.—8 18-inch spokes of No. 4 rattan,
　　　　　　　1 10-inch spoke of No. 4 rattan,
　　　　　　　6 weavers of No. 2 rattan,
　　　　　　　½ weaver of No. 2 rattan stained green.
　　　　HANDLE.—6 32-inch pieces of No. 2 rattan,
　　　　　　　A knitting needle.

A slightly concave bottom is woven, on eight and a half spokes, to a diameter of two and a half inches; when the spokes are soaked until pliable and then turned up with a very slight flare, to about an inch from the bottom. Here six pieces of No. 2 rattan thirty-two inches long are inserted, three on either side of a spoke, with the help of a knitting needle, which is first run down to make room for the ends. These six pieces are then braided into a handle (having two pieces in each strand) of the desired height. The ends are pushed down, three on each side of a spoke, directly opposite the one where the handle was started and the weaving of the basket continues. The half weaver in green is divided again and woven into one row of double weave; then the spokes are wet and bent outward, until they are so flared as almost to be horizontal. The weaver must be pushed back to make it loose enough to allow the spokes to spread. The flare continues for almost two inches, when the basket is bound off and finished with Open Border No. 2. This, if the loops are low, not over five-eighths of an inch from the weaving, will make an appropriate and pretty finish.

Baby's Rattle with Handle of Rattan and Cane

Materials: RATTLE.—4 26-inch spokes of No. 3 rattan,
1 14-inch spoke of No. 3 rattan,
3½ weavers of No. 2 rattan,
4 small round bells.
HANDLE.—1 length of fine split cane.

The spokes are bound and the weaving begun in the usual way except that from the centre the spokes are bent up and out, making a rounding top to the rattle. This flare continues until at two and a half inches from the centre the circumference is a little over ten inches. The weaver is then pulled more tightly, drawing in the spokes at first gradually and then decidedly until they almost meet, when four small bells are slipped in, and the weaving continued as far as it will go. All but one of the spokes are cut to a length of four inches from the last row of weaving, that one being left nine inches long. A length of fine cane such as is used in caning chairs, see Chapter XIII, is next wet for a few minutes and, after the spokes of the handle have been laid in proper order, it is started as close to the end of the weaving as possible, with its end turning down along the handle.

The handle is held so that the spokes will not twist, and the cane is wound around it evenly and tightly, edge to edge, so that none of the rattan shows. At an inch and a quarter from the end of the handle, the long spoke is bent over into a loop and the end pressed up among the other spokes. The winding then continues to the end of the handle, and around the loop in the same way, until it is covered, when the cane is cut off leaving an end an inch long. This end is woven up the handle, over and under several rows of cane. When it has been woven in this way for about half an inch, it is bent back and run down under the cane. This finishes a rattle which a child can easily weave, and it will delight him to find he is able to make such an acceptable little gift for a baby brother or sister.

Vase-Shaped Basket with Ring Handles

Materials: BASKET.—8 20-inch spokes of No. 3 terra cotta rattan,
  1 11-inch spoke of No. 3 terra cotta rattan,
  5 weavers of No. 2 terra cotta rattan.
  HANDLES.—2 23-inch pieces of No. 4 rattan stained black to within two inches of each end,
  A knitting needle.

HANDLES

The fine spokes that are used in this basket make it easier to mold into curves than if it was woven on the more rigid, heavy spoke material. A terra cotta stain, see Chapter XII, is used to color the spokes and weavers of this basket, and two pieces of No 4 rattan twenty-three inches long are stained black to within two inches of each end, to form the ring shaped handles on the sides. A concave bottom, two and three-quarters inches in diameter, is woven; the spokes are then wet and the sides turned up to form a bowl shape. After the second weaver has been used the spokes are gradually drawn in by tightening the weavers, until the fifth weaver is started; when the spokes are gradually flared, until three-quarters of the fifth weaver has been used. Then they are more flared until the end of the fifth weaver is reached, when the basket is bound off. In the border each spoke is brought over the next one on the right, back of the next and then out where it is cut slanting just long enough to allow it to lie across the next spoke on the right.

Ring handles are made in the same way as the rings described on page 39, only on a much larger scale, being almost three and a half inches in diameter. They are twisted so that the rings will be made of the stained part of the rattan; leaving the plain ends to be woven under and over where the rings are attached, (one on each side of the basket under the third row of weaving from the top) and afterward colored with the terra cotta stain.

Basket with Twisted Handle having Interlaced Ends

Materials: BASKET.—8 20-inch spokes of No. 4 rattan,
1 11-inch spoke of No. 4 rattan,
6 weavers of No. 2 rattan.
HANDLE.—1 length of No. 4 rattan.

A bottom is woven two and three-quarters inches in diameter, on eight and a half twenty-inch spokes, which are then thoroughly wet and bent upward with a slight flare. When two weavers have been used, the spokes are flared more decidedly, and when two more have been woven in this way, the spokes are drawn in while using the remaining two weavers. The edge is then bound off and finished with the simple border described in the directions for a basket with a twisted handle in the first part of the chapter.

Handle.—A length of No. 4 rattan which has been soaked until pliable is cut into four pieces and then separated into pairs. These are bent into loops at about ten inches from one end of each and knotted in this way. The loops are held firmly where the short end of each comes against the long end, (making sure that the short ends are on the

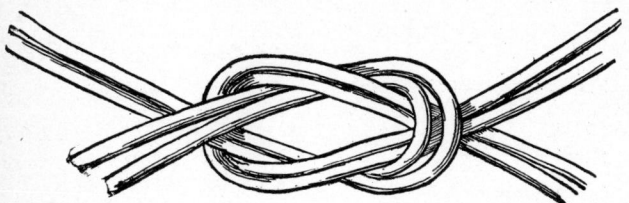

FIG. 13

same sides of the loops) one in each hand of the worker, who passes one loop through the other, bringing the ends of the loop through which it passed over it, which makes the loop uppermost on one end of the knot and on the other the ends, see Fig. 13. The short ends are now crossed one under a long end and one over (as shown in Fig. 13), and brought

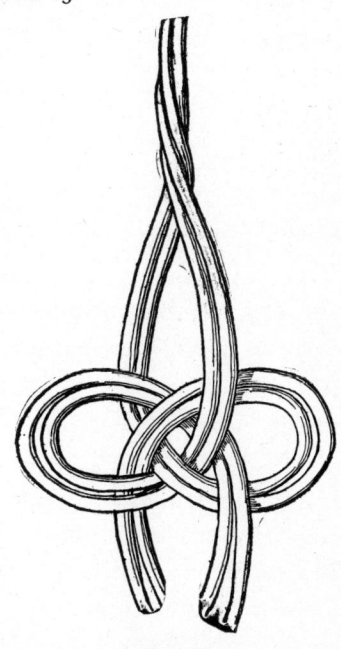

FIG. 14

together. The long ends are also brought together making a knot like Fig. 14. This knot is placed about half way between the top and bottom of the basket, with the long ends turning up. The short ends are finished off by weaving one to the right over and under several spokes and the other to the left. The long ends are twisted together for about twelve inches, and are then made into another knot copied from the first one for, although the process cannot be the same, it is so simple that one can easily follow its coils. This knot is placed on the opposite side of the basket from the first one and attached in the same way

Work Baskets

CHAPTER VII

WORK BASKETS

As almost everyone who uses a work basket has a different ideal of what such a basket should be—in regard to size, capacity, shape and ornament—these descriptions are not to be taken as directions, but as suggestions which each basket maker can adapt or elaborate upon. In this way he can work out a basket suited to the taste and needs of the person by whom it is to be used.

Small Bowl Shaped Work Basket

Materials: 10 22-inch spokes of No. 4 rattan,
1 12-inch spoke of No. 4 rattan,
7 weavers of No. 2 rattan.

A small open work basket which is pretty and serviceable, though simple, is made as follows: Two groups of spokes, one of five and the other of five and a half, are crossed in the centre in the usual way and bound around three times with a weaver of No. 2 rattan, which is woven in under-and-over weaving to a diameter of three and a half inches, when the spokes are wet and turned very gradually upward in a rounding flare. When three weavers and part of a fourth have been used, a fifth weaver is started beside the fourth in double weaving, which continues for five rows. The weavers are still left loose enough for the spokes to flare, and when the band of double weaving is finished, and an inch of under-and-over weaving has been made above it, the diameter of the top should be seven and five-eighths inches. It is then bound off and finished with the Rope Border described on page 39. The whole basket may be colored with a vegetable dye or stain, (see Chapter XII) or the band of double weaving may be woven with colored rattan, the rest of the basket being of rattan in its natural color. As the border ends inside and as there are also many little ends of weavers on the inside which would be troublesome in a work basket, a lining of silk in some harmonious color, with pockets and pin-cushion, will make it more practical.

Travelling Work Basket of Raffia and Rattan

Materials: BASKET—16 18-inch pieces of No. 2 rattan,
11 or 12 lengths of colored raffia,
1½ weavers of No. 1 rattan.
COVER AND HINGE—16 16-inch pieces of No. 2 rattan,
7 or 8 lengths of colored raffia,
½ weaver of No. 1 rattan.

A dainty little work basket just large enough to hold a small pair of scissors, needles, thread and a thimble will be a welcome gift to some globe-trotting friend. Before beginning it a bunch of raffia should be dyed a pale color that will look well with the rattan, see Chapter XII. Such a fine rattan as No. 1 is not always obtainable, it is so seldom used, but in a tiny basket like this no heavier material will look as well. The sixteen eighteen-inch pieces of No. 2 rattan are separated into groups of four each. The first group is laid on a table in a vertical position. Across the centre of this group the second group is placed horizontally exactly at its centre, the third group crosses the other two diagonally with its upper end to the right of the upper part of the vertical group and its centre over the point where the other two cross. The fourth group is laid across the others diagonally, from the left of the upper part of the vertical group to the right of the lower part. A length of raffia is then doubled and started around the upper part of the vertical group, with its ends toward the right. It is woven in pairing to about seven-eighths of an inch from the centre, where the groups are divided, each making two groups containing two pieces of rattan. When a bottom two and a half inches in diameter, and slightly raised in the centre, has been woven the groups of spokes are thoroughly wet and turned up with a slight flare, using a No. 1 weaver in four rows of pairing. This is succeeded by seven-eighths of an inch of raffia in pairing, which flares for three quarters of an inch and is then drawn in gradually. In joining the ends of two weavers of raffia, two inches at least of the old and new weaver should be laid one on top of the other, twisted tightly together and woven as one strand; this will make a neater joining than crossing the ends back of a spoke. The band of four rows of pairing in No. 1 rattan which follows the raffia is also drawn in gradually, making a firm edge at the top of the basket. The groups of spokes are then wet and woven into a border which looks like a plait, and is made in this way. Each group of two spokes is brought back of the next group on the right, in front of the next and down inside the basket just behind the third group to the right of it. As usual in this kind of a closed border the first part of the border should be left loose and open until the last part has been woven in.

Cover.—The same arrangement of groups of spokes is made in starting the cover as in the bottom of the basket, and it is woven in pairing with weavers of raffia, turning the spokes up from the very centre so as to make a slightly rounded cover. At seven-eighths of an inch from the centre the groups of four are divided into twos, and the pairing with raffia continues until the cover is three inches in diameter. Two rows of pairing in No. 1 rattan follow the raffia and they are succeeded by a single row of raffia and a border like the one on the basket. The hinge and fastening are made of raffia and rattan. Three strands of raffia sixteen inches long are braided and then cut into two pieces; one to form the hinge and the other the top loop of the fastening. The hinge is made by inserting one end of the braided raffia under a loop of the border to the left of a group of spokes on the basket. It is brought outside of the basket on the right of the group of spokes. Both ends are now on the outside of the basket and after placing the cover on the basket, to see where it will fit best, the ends are brought straight up, each over a lower loop in the border of the cover and one on either side of a group of spokes, to the inside of the cover. Here the ends of the braid are crossed and woven to right and left, under and over one or two spokes, to fasten them off.

In the front of the cover an end of the other eight inch piece of braided raffia is pushed through to the inside, on the left of a group of spokes, and just above a lower loop of the border. The other end is brought inside to the right of the group of spokes; the ends are then drawn up until the loop on the outside is about an inch long, when they are crossed and woven to right and left under and over one or two spokes to fasten them securely. A piece of No. 1 rattan, about twelve inches long, is fastened to the basket just below the loop on the cover and between the lowest row in the band of rattan and the top of the woven raffia. It is brought up vertically and pushed inside the basket just below the border, making the foundation for a rattan loop which is formed in the same way as the small side handles described on page 55. Over this rattan loop the loop of braided raffia fits, and a piece of No. 5 rattan an inch long is slipped through the rattan loop and holds the cover close. That it may not be lost, a hole is bored in this piece of rattan and it is fastened to the basket by a bit of raffia; one end of which is tied through the hole in the rattan, the other secured around a spoke about an inch to the right of the fastening.

The finishing touch of daintiness is to line this basket with silk, and fit into the hollow in the cover a round needle-book made of the same silk.

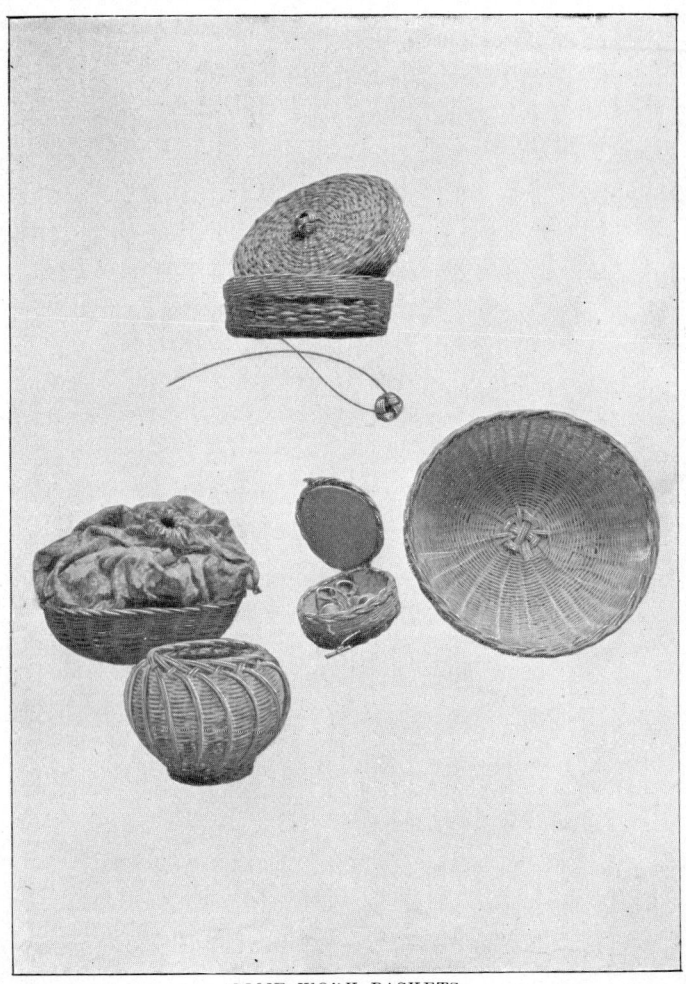

SOME WORK BASKETS

The round knitting basket in the foreground is of rattan in the natural color, as is the large bowl-shaped basket on the right. In the centre is a small travelling work basket of pale green raffia, and on the left a green rattan basket with a soft silk top. Above is shown the Chinese button or knob which is used on the green rush covered basket

Large Bowl Shaped Work Basket

Materials: 16 34-inch pieces of No. 2 rattan,
32 17-inch pieces of No. 2 rattan,
11 or more weavers of No. 2 rattan,
A knitting needle.

The thirty-four-inch pieces of No. 2 rattan are arranged in groups of four and crossed in the centre as described on page 67. A single weaver is started by laying the end over the group to the left of the upper end of the vertical group, it is then brought under the vertical group, over the next, under the next and so on, until it comes around to the vertical group again. Here it goes under as before, over the next group and always under and over the same groups as at first. The weaver is

FIG 15

brought around four times in this way, see Fig. 15. The groups are now separated into twos, and the weaver is brought over the left hand pair of the upper vertical group, under the pair on the right, and so on until it comes around again when it is brought under and over the same groups as in the row just completed, see Fig. 15. When the fourth row has been made in this way, another weaver is added, by inserting it between a group of spokes and the band of weaving which covers them, and the pairing of which the rest of the basket is to be woven is begun. The centre being woven in a design, is so ornamental that rather than cover it with a lining, which would be necessary if the usual

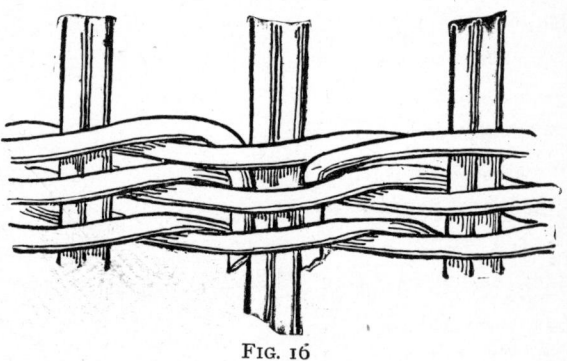

FIG. 16

method of joining weavers was followed, the end of each old weaver is run down between the weaving, on the left of a group of spokes, and the end of the new weaver is run down between the weaving to the right of the same group, see Fig. 16. When the bottom of the basket is five and a half inches in diameter, pieces of No. 2 rattan seventeen inches long are inserted, one on either side of every group of spokes, making four pieces of rattan in each group. These are again divided into pairs and spread apart. When the bottom is six inches in diameter, the groups of spokes are wet and bent gradually upward. The basket is woven into a bowl shape with flaring sides, and, when about eleven weavers have been used, the top should be ten inches in diameter. The ends of the groups of spokes are woven into a border as follows: In the first row each group is brought under the next one to the right, over the next, under the next and outside of the basket. In the second row each end of a group is brought under the next end on the right, over the next and then pressed inside the basket just behind the third group of spokes from where it started. The third row is made by bringing each end across one group of spokes and then outside of the basket, where it is cut just long enough to allow it to lie across the next group.

Covered Work Basket of Green Rush

Materials: BASKET—10 20-inch spokes of No. 4 rattan,
   1 11-inch spoke of No. 4 rattan,
   4 weavers of No. 2 rattan,
   Flat green rush.
COVER AND KNOB.— 8 20-inch spokes of No. 4 rattan,
   1 11-inch spoke of No. 4 rattan,
   16 10-inch spokes of No. 4 rattan,
   4½ weavers of No. 2 rattan,
   Flat green rush,
   A knitting needle.

In weaving with rush or raffia, but especially with rush, it is impossible to give the number of pieces necessary to make a basket, because of the varying length and thickness of the material. A caution will not be out of place in regard to soaking the rush. It should be wet just long enough to prevent its breaking when woven. As it is a very porous material it absorbs so much moisture if left too long in water that it shrinks badly when dry, and a basket that was quite firm when woven may become loose and shaky after the rush is dry. It follows of course that rush baskets should be very tightly woven, each weaver pressed down on those already in place, and sometimes, after the sides are finished, the weaving is bound down with string or linen thread (passed between the spokes and across the basket) and left to get perfectly dry before the border is made. In beginning this basket two groups of spokes, one of five and one of five and a half, are crossed in the centre. A weaver of green rush is bound around them and woven in under-and-over weaving into a bottom six and three-quarters inches in diameter which is slightly raised in the centre. The spokes are then wet until quite pliable, and turned sharply upward, with three rows of triple twist, to begin the straight sides of the basket. Next an inch and a quarter of rush is woven in under-and-over weaving, and five-eighths of an inch of triple twist forms a firm band at the top, which is completed with this border. Each spoke in turn is brought in front of the spoke on the left and down inside the basket, where it is cut off after the border is finished.

Cover.—The cover is woven of rush, on groups of four and four and a half spokes, until a centre four inches in diameter is made, when sixteen extra spokes are inserted, from the under side, one on the right of each spoke but one. The ends of these spokes are held in place by a row of pairing in rush, the spokes being separated as it is woven around. The under-and-over weaving with rush then continues until the cover is seven and three-quarters inches in diameter. The spokes should next be thoroughly wet and turned sharply up, to make the straight sides, which are woven in triple twist for an inch and a quarter. In ending the last row of triple twist the following process will be found more satisfactory than the usual one. When the weaving reaches the point on the circumference of the basket where it began, each of the three ends is cut about an inch and a quarter beyond the last spoke behind which it was brought. Each end is then pressed down on the left of the next spoke and between the weaving. The border is a simple one. Each spoke is brought back of the next spoke on the left and out, where it is cut slanting just long enough to allow it to lie across the succeeding spoke.

Knob.—A curious little button or knob, by which to lift the cover, is copied from one on a Chinese basket, and is made of a piece of No. 2 rattan, about half a length. The rattan is soaked until very pliable and then bent into a loop, like the one on the right of Fig. 17, leaving an end about four inches long. This loop should be a little over an inch across the widest part. The long end of the rattan is bent into another loop of the same size, the end being brought under the short end and up again, see Fig. 17; passing over the left side of the second loop, under the left side of the first loop, over the right side of the second loop, under the right side of the first loop

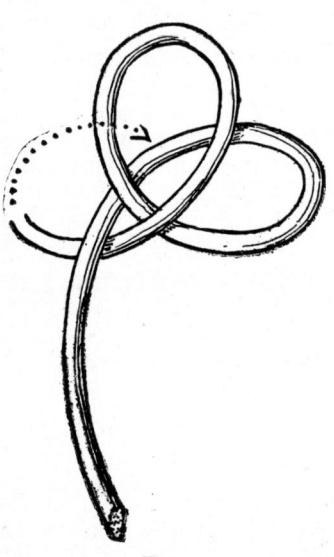

FIG. 17

and around to the right or inside of the short end, see Fig. 18. Here having made one circuit it follows the first circuit exactly, close to it and always on the inside. When the weaver has gone around four times it will have formed a little button or knob, with a small opening at the top and a larger one underneath ; especially if the worker keeps this form in mind as he molds the rattan. The knob is attached to the centre of the cover by its two ends.

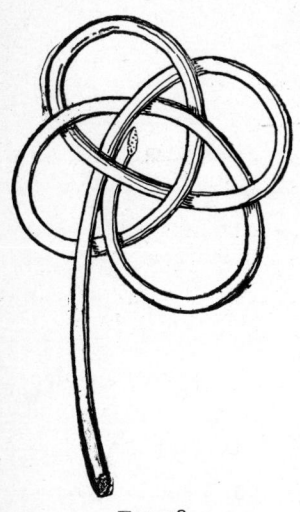

FIG. 18

Napkin Ring

Material: 1 length of No. 4 rattan.

A length of heavier rattan may be made into a simple and most useful napkin ring, for summer cottages or camps, by following the directions for the Chinese knob with but one difference. In making the second circuit, the beginning of which is shown in Fig. 18, the long end is brought on the left or outside of the short end and continues around on that side. Five circuits may be made instead of four if the ring does not seem firm enough at the end of the fourth. The ring form

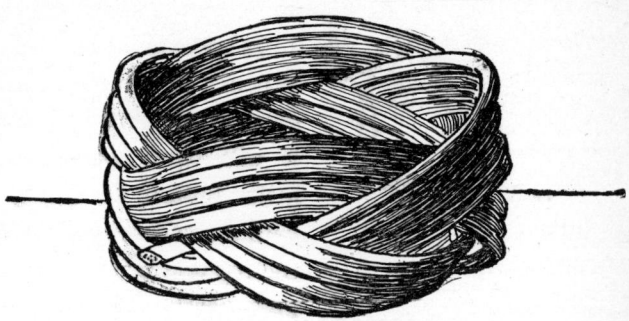

Fig. 19.—Napkin Ring

must of course be in mind all the time, so that it shall be molded into that instead of the knob shape. It may be finished in the natural color or stained (see Chapter XII).

Knitting Basket

Materials: 16 32-inch pieces of No. 2 rattan,
10 weavers of No. 2 rattan,
A knitting needle.

Here is something to make for the friend who knits or crochets; a little round basket that will hold her ball and needles and the piece of work too, if it is not very large. The sixteen pieces of

No. 2 rattan are separated into groups of four each, which are crossed in the Indian way already described on page 67. Three rows of pairing are woven in No. 2 rattan, and then the groups are separated into twos, and the pairing continues while the basket is shaped as nearly round as possible. That there may be no ends of weavers inside the basket, to catch on the work, the method of joining weavers described on page 72 is used. At the widest point, when half of the fifth weaver has been woven in, the circumference should be about sixteen and three-quarters inches; from there it is gradually drawn in until, when the ninth weaver has been used, the diameter of the top is about four and a half inches. Each group of spokes is then brought over the next two groups on the right, back of the third group and outside. When this row is finished each group is brought down to the bottom of the basket on the outside, to a point an inch and a quarter from the centre and just in front of the next spoke to the one it last went behind, where it is drawn through two rows of weaving to hold it in place. These outside groups should be left quite loose as will be seen in the picture. When this process is finished (and a knitting needle will be a great help in accomplishing it) the basket is turned upside down and two rows of pairing are made to form part of a base; the end of each group is then brought over the next end to the right and pressed down inside (where they are afterward cut short), completing the base.

Candy Baskets

CHAPTER VIII

CANDY BASKETS

CHILDREN will delight in weaving baskets of this kind, and with the fine grades of rattan, with rush in its beautiful natural shades, and raffia which takes color so well, the possibilities for dainty little favors and effective larger baskets are endless.

Candy Basket of Rattan with a Band of Color

Materials: 10 20-inch spokes of No. 4 rattan,
1 11-inch spoke of No. 4 rattan,
5 weavers of No. 2 rattan,
2 weavers of No. 2 colored rattan.

Two weavers of colored rattan, dyed according to one of the descriptions in Chapter XII, form the band on this basket, which is woven, in a simple Indian shape, of rattan in the natural color. Two groups of spokes, one of five and the other of five and a half, are crossed in the centre and bound around three times with No. 2 rattan which is woven in under-and-over weaving into a flat bottom, about six and a quarter inches in diameter. The spokes are then wet thoroughly and turned up, rounding them gradually. After about a quarter of an inch has been woven up the sides, two colored weavers are woven into four rows of double weaving, which are drawn in slightly toward the top; three rows of under-and-over weaving in No. 2 rattan are also slightly drawn in, and then the top is bound off and finished with this border. Each spoke is brought back of the next one on the right, in front of the next, back of the next and then out, taking special care to leave the first spokes loose so that the last ones can be easily woven in. They are then cut slanting just long enough to allow each to lie across the spoke in front of it.

Brown Rush Candy Basket with Overlapping Cover

Materials: BASKET.—8 18-inch spokes of No. 4 rattan,
1 10-inch spoke of No. 4 rattan,
16 9-inch spokes of No. 4 rattan,
5 weavers of No. 2 rattan,
Flat brown rush.
COVER AND HANDLE—8 16-inch spokes of No. 4 rattan,
1 9-inch spoke of No. 4 rattan,
16 8-inch spokes of No. 4 rattan,
1 12-inch spoke of No. 4 rattan,
5 weavers of No. 2 rattan,
Flat brown rush,
A knitting needle.

The soft shades of brown in the rush, combined with rattan in its natural color, harmonize beautifully in this basket which, after it has been used for candy, may be lined and transformed into a work basket that will last for years. The eighteen-inch spokes, in groups of four and four and a half, are crossed in the centre and a length of brown rush, previously wet until pliable, is bound about them in this way: The end is started back of the upper vertical spokes and lying along the horizontal ones, with the tip toward the right. It is then brought in front of the upper vertical spokes, down back of the horizontal ones to the right, in front of the lower vertical ones, then diagonally up back of the centre to the space between the upper vertical spokes and the horizontal ones on the right; next in front of the horizontal ones on the right, diagonally up across the back of the centre to the space to the left of the upper vertical spokes. Then down in front of the horizontal spokes on the left, and back to the space on the right of the upper vertical spokes, where the spokes are separated and the weaving begins. A centre three and three-quarters inches in diameter is woven of rush, then the extra sixteen spokes are inserted, one to the right of every spoke but one, on the wrong side of the work, and two rows of triple twist in No. 2 rattan holds them firmly in place and covers the joining. Four rows of rush are woven, and the spokes are wet until perfectly pliable, when they are turned sharply up and the weaving of the sides is begun with half an inch of triple twist. Five rows of rush in under-and-over weaving follow and then five-eighths of an inch of triple twist makes a firm band at the top. The border is a simple one, finished inside so as to allow the cover to slip on and off easily. Each spoke is brought in front of the next one to the left and down inside.

Cover.—In making the cover the spokes are crossed and bound as they were in the basket. A centre, four and three-quarters inches in diameter, is woven with the rush; the sixteen extra spokes are then inserted, as in the basket, and bound firmly with two rows of triple twist. Five rows of rush are woven in under-and-over weaving and then the spokes are thoroughly wet and bent up sharply. Five-eighths of an inch of triple twist in No. 2 weavers makes an overlapping edge, which should be perfectly straight and true. In ending the triple twist the method described on page 75 is recommended. A border is made by bringing each spoke back of the one on the left and then out. A small handle by which to lift the cover is formed of a piece of No. 4 rattan. It is started by weaving it under and over two or three spokes near the centre, bringing the long end up on the outside, between two of the centre spokes just beyond the binding, and down on the opposite side of the centre, beyond the place where it is bound with the rush. It is brought across again and then woven under and over several spokes to fasten it. This makes two loops of rattan both about half an inch high and lying close together. An end of very pliable rush is now started at one end of this foundation handle, on the right of it, and brought over and around the left loop, then out between the loops, around the right loop, out again between the loops and around the left. This is repeated until the rattan is entirely covered with rush (the stitches pressed close together), making a handle which is quite in keeping with the rest of the basket.

Open Work Candy Basket

Materials: 24 30-inch pieces of No. 2 rattan,
2 weavers of No. 2 rattan.

This basket is a popular one, not at all difficult to make, and with a pretty little lace paper doily by way of a lining it holds candy very well. The twenty-four pieces of rattan, previously soaked until pliable, are separated into groups of six each which are arranged in the Indian way described on page 67. A weaver of No. 2 rattan is doubled around the upper end of the vertical group, with its ends toward the right. It is woven in two rows of pairing, starting at about an inch from the centre. A third row of pairing is then woven, dividing each group into groups of three each. The ends of the weavers are finished off by cutting them, at about an inch beyond the end of the third row of pairing, and pushing each through a loop in the weaving on the wrong side, to hold it fast. Each group of three spokes is then brought over the next group on the right, under the following one, over the next, under the next and outside down by the weaving, making a loop about two and a half inches high and some long ends of each group. The first loops especially, should be left loose, so that the last two or three groups can be easily finished off. When this mat has been made even on all sides, by pulling the loops out or drawing them in, it is molded up into a bowl shape with the hands. It is then placed, top downward, on the worker's knee and a weaver of No. 2 rattan doubled in the centre is started, around the end of a group, at the point on the circumference of the basket where the first pairing ended. Three rows of pairing are woven to make the beginning of a base, taking care not to draw in the groups too much, but to keep the sides of the base straight. The end of each group is then brought over the next group on the left, and pressed down inside the base, where it is cut off afterward.

Flat Candy Basket with Braided Handle

Materials: BASKET.—16 20-inch pieces of No. 2 rattan,
                    3 weavers of No. 2 rattan.
          HANDLE.— 6 22-inch pieces of No. 2 rattan,
                    A knitting needle.

This basket makes a charming little favor for luncheon or dinner. A small paper doily with a lace edge may be laid inside and the candy arranged upon it. The centre is started with sixteen twenty-inch pieces of No. 2 rattan, separated into four groups of four each, and crossed in the Indian manner already described on page 67. The weaver is started in front of the group to the left of the upper vertical group. It then goes back of the upper vertical group, in front of the next group, back of the next and so on, until one row has been made. In the second, third and fourth rows the weaver is brought under and over the same groups as in the first row, but in the next row it is first brought back of the upper vertical group and the group on the right of it, then in front of the next group, back of the next and so on. Four rows are woven in this way and then the groups of four are divided into twos and the weaver is brought over the first group of two on the right of the upper vertical group, under the second, and so on. The next row is woven under and over the same groups, but at the end of that row the weaver is brought behind two groups, and the weave changes again. It is now in groups of two weavers crossing two spokes, and continues in this way till the basket is finished. New weavers are joined to the old by whittling the end of each to a flat point two or three inches long. These points are held close together and woven along like a whole weaver. When the bottom is about four and three-quarters inches in diameter, a braided handle is made and inserted according to the description in Chapter VI, using six pieces of No. 2 weaver twenty-two inches long. When the bottom is five and three-eighths inches in diameter the groups of spokes are wet and turned up to form the sides, which are not over half an inch high. The border is the same as the one described on page 68, only it is drawn in very tightly so as to make the plait lie almost flat. This basket may be colored with a vegetable dye, according to the directions in Chapter XII, or it may be left the natural color of the rattan.

CANDY BASKETS

Covered Basket with Hinge, Handle and Fastening in One

Materials: BASKET—6 22-inch spokes of No. 4 rattan,
1 12-inch spoke of No. 4 rattan,
4 weavers of No. 2 rattan.
COVER, HINGE, ETC.—6 18-inch spokes of No. 4 rattan,
1 10-inch spoke of No. 4 rattan,
3½ weavers of No. 2 rattan,
A knitting needle.

What makes this basket unusual and attractive is the hinge, top-handle and fastening, which are all formed of one weaver in a series of twists. The basket and cover are simply made. Two groups of spokes, twenty-two inches long, one of three, and the other of three and a half, are crossed in the centre, bound three times around, and woven into a bottom two and a half inches in diameter. The spokes are then wet and bent upward with a decided flare which, when four weavers have been used, should make the diameter of the top about five inches. It is then bound off and finished with this border. Each spoke in turn is brought back of the next spoke on the right, in front of the next, back of the next, in front of the next, and pressed down inside the basket. This being such a deep border, the first part of it should be left loose and open, that the last spokes may be fitted into place without any trouble. It should be remembered in weaving in these last spokes that each time a spoke crosses another it goes one row farther down in the border, until at last it lies on the weaving.

Cover.—The cover is begun like the bottom of the basket, except that it is flared up and out from the very centre. Two weavers are used, and toward the end of the second the spokes are flared until they lie in a horizontal position. When the diameter is five and a quarter inches the edge is bound off and finished with the Rope Border described on page 39.

Hinge, Top Handle and Fastening.—A weaver of No. 2 rattan is cut into fourths, these are then separated into pairs, which are doubled at the centre and knotted according to the directions on page 61. This knot is drawn up until it is about two inches across. It is then placed in the centre of the cover with the ends extending over the front and back of the basket. The pairs of ends which are toward the back of the basket are crossed, the left being the upper one, and they are pressed down through the cover, one on either side of a spoke, and between the last row of weaving and the border. Each pair is now brought through a loop in the centre of the border of the basket,

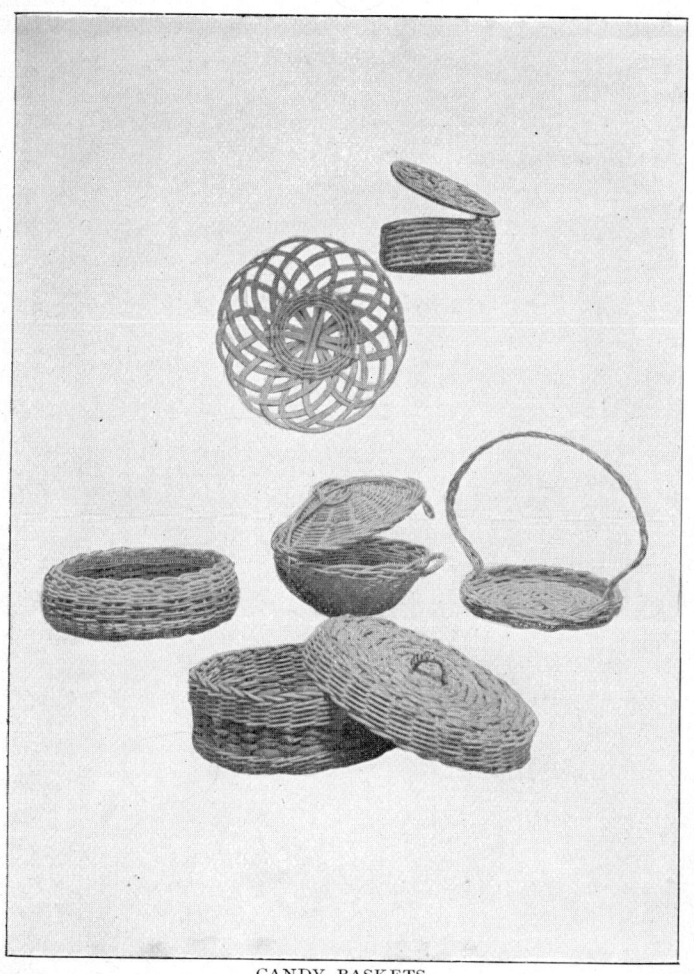

CANDY BASKETS

In the foreground is the brown rush and rattan covered basket; directly above it a smaller basket with elaborate hinge, top handle and fastenings is placed. At the left is an attractive Indian shape ornamented with a pale-green band. The shallow basket on the right makes a charming favor for a dinner or cotillon

and after crossing again (the right over the left), they are fastened off, one on either side of a spoke at about half an inch from the bottom. The hinge and top handle are then completed. To make the cover fastening, the pairs of ends toward the front are crossed (the right over the left), and brought down between the first and second rows of weaving from the edge, one on either side of a spoke. They are crossed again at about an inch and a half below the edge of the cover (the left over the right) to make the beginning of a loop. The end on the right is now brought up, back of the right side of the loop and through it, while the end on the left is brought up and over the left side of the loop. They cross in the middle of the loop near the edge of the cover (the right being uppermost) and are finished off, one on each side of the spoke, and between the border and the last row of weaving on the cover. A larger ring on the basket forms the other part of the fastening, and is made as follows: Two pieces of No. 2 weaver, sixteen inches long, are laid together and bent into a loop at about an inch from the middle (the ends turning down) by crossing the right pair of ends over the left. Those on the left are then brought under the left side of the ring and out, while the other pair are brought over the right side of the ring and in, completing a ring which should be just large enough for the loop on the cover to pass through. The ends are inserted, one pair on either side of a spoke, in the front of the basket, where they cross and are woven to right and left between the sixth and seventh rows of weaving below the border, or just where the loop on the cover will pass through the ring and form a fastening.

Basket of Coiled Rattan Wound and Decorated with Raffia

Materials: BASKET—1 length of No. 4 rattan,
A bunch of raffia,
A bunch of orange raffia,
A bunch of black raffia,
A tapestry needle, No. 19.
COVER AND HINGE—½ a length of No. 4 rattan,
A bunch of raffia,
A bunch of orange raffia,
A bunch of black raffia.

Time and patience might be added to the above list, for it will take a good stock of both to make this basket. The result, however, should be pretty and original enough to compensate for it all. A length of No. 4 rattan is soaked until pliable. The end is then coiled into the smallest possible ring and a needleful of raffia is started, with the end toward the right, in the centre of the ring, and sewed over

CANDY BASKETS

and over from left to right with a tapestry needle. The next coil is brought around at a little distance (about the width of No. 4 rattan) from the first one and, when a quarter of the second row of coiling has been made, the raffia is brought down through the centre, up and round once again, thus holding the first coil to the second by a joining, which is made more secure by binding it twice around with the raffia in the opposite direction to the way it is wound around the rattan. When the coil has been brought half way around the second time another of these joinings is made. There is another one when three-quarters of the row has been coiled, and still another at the beginning of the third row of coiling. The next joining should be just to the right of the first one, and from that on, each row is joined to the next at the right of the joinings on the previous row. Thus these joinings form a pattern, like the spokes in the all rattan baskets, and answering the same purpose. As the coils grow larger the number of joinings must of course be increased, for the same reason that extra spokes are inserted in weaving, to keep the work firm. This is done by putting one between each of the other joinings. New needlefuls of raffia are always started at a joining. The needle brings the end of the old strand from left to right, through the upper part of the joining, leaving the end lying along the under side of the rattan. The new needleful is then brought from right to left through two twists of the raffia and drawn up so as to leave a short end lying along the rattan. The winding then begins again and soon

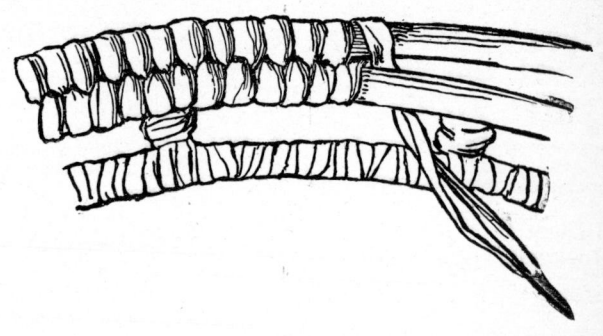

FIG. 20

covers both ends. At the end of the tenth coil the rattan is brought up directly above that coil, leaving the same distance between the new coil and the one below it as there was between the other coils. Each coil now follows just above the previous one—making a straight-sided basket, eight coils high. The ninth coil is brought just inside the eighth, in order to make a little rim for the cover to rest upon. In making the ninth coil, when about two and a quarter inches from the point on the circumference of the basket where the coil was brought up to form the sides, the rattan should be cut just long enough to complete the row and whittled to a long, flat point, which is sewed close to the previous row of coiling.

Cover.—The cover is wound and coiled in the same way as the bottom of the basket as far as the end of the ninth row of coiling, when a border is made by bringing the tenth row close to the ninth with the stitch shown in Fig. 20. The extreme end of the rattan is whittled to a long point and sewed in with the previous row.

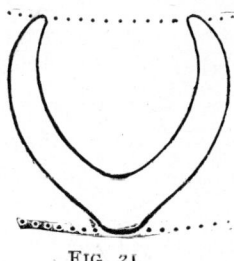

FIG. 21

The designs on the basket and cover are worked before they are fastened together. Beginning with the basket—the circumference is divided into fifths, and a line of black thread is run from top to bottom of the basket, at each of the five points, to form a centre line for the petal-shaped design shown in Fig. 21. The design may also be outlined in black basting thread or done by eye, in stitches which run under and over the coils like weaving, except that the raffia is brought *through* the previous row each time (instead of simply crossing it) between the coils. The design on the model was first worked in orange raffia, and then outlined inside with two rows of black. The design on the cover is like a five-petalled flower (see Fig. 22), and after it has been worked, the cover is placed on the basket so that the end of each petal will come in the space between two of the petals on the basket.

FIG. 22

Hinge.—The place where the hinge is to be made on the basket having been decided upon, a ring of raffia is formed by sewing a strand twice around the last two rows of coiling at the left of a joining, and covering it with button-hole stitch in raffia. Another ring is made on the right of the joining in the same way. At a point on the cover, just above the ring on the right, a needleful of raffia is attached, run through the rings and then around the last row of coiling on the border. It is drawn up until it forms a loop just loose enough to allow the cover to open easily, when it is covered with button-hole stitch.

Scrap Baskets

CHAPTER IX

SCRAP BASKETS

THERE is always a demand for a strong, practical scrap basket, and if it is a thing of beauty so much the better. Simple forms are the best, and the study of Indian baskets will help the workman in his choice. The straight-sided scrap basket is one of the most satisfactory if the material used is attractive and the weaving well done.

Rattan and Rush Scrap Basket

Materials: A bunch of braided green rush,
8 44-inch spokes of No. 5 rattan,
1 23-inch spoke of No. 5 rattan,
16 22-inch spokes of No. 5 rattan,
16 weavers of No. 3 rattan,
A knife,
A knitting needle.

In using such heavy spokes as No. 5 it will be hard to make a flat bottom unless, instead of the usual arrangement, the horizontal spokes are slit in the centre for about an inch, or just far enough to slip the vertical spokes through them. The weaver is then started behind the upper vertical spokes in the usual way, and bound three times around before beginning to weave. When the bottom is about four inches in diameter, the sixteen short spokes, previously sharpened to a point, are inserted, one on the right of each of the spokes, except one (to keep the uneven number), which is closer than the others. The spokes are then evenly separated, and the weaving proceeds till the bottom is eight inches in diameter, when the spokes should be wet until pliable, and then turned sharply upward. An inch of triple twist forms a band at the base. Just here it may be said that all ornamental weaving, or weaving done with wide material, like rush, should begin and end at the same point on the circumference of the basket. If not, as will readily be seen, the basket will be uneven at the top. The rush, which has been soaked for fifteen or twenty minutes, is now started behind a spoke and woven in under-and-over weaving for eight inches. If it is necessary to join the rush at any time, the ends should be crossed behind a spoke and sewed firmly together with silk matching the dull green of the rush. In this basket it will take care to keep the sides straight and true, and the spokes at an even distance apart. Constant criticism of the work from a distance is

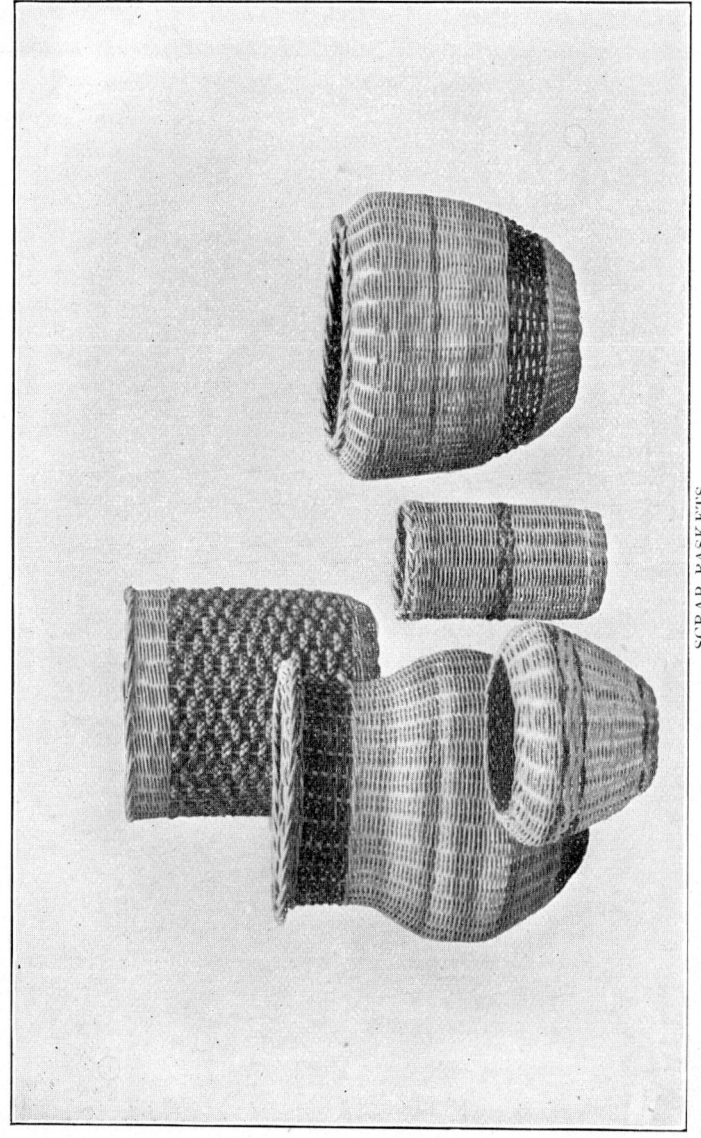

SCRAP BASKETS

The two small scrap baskets in the foreground are for use on a table or desk. They, as well as the two large baskets near them, are of rattan with bands of color. The large basket in the background is of dull green rush.

the only sure way to make such large baskets symmetrical. There are two inches of triple twist at the top, which makes a firm rim, and the basket is finished with the following border: After the spokes have been soaked until quite pliable, a small piece is cut out of the right side of each one, close to the weaving. This acts as a hinge, preventing the spokes breaking when they are bent sharply down. This border is in two rows; that is, the circuit of the basket is made twice, each time using a different process.

In the first row each spoke is brought back of two spokes and then out.

In the second row the end of each spoke is brought under two ends, and then pushed down inside the basket under the third end, and just back of an upright spoke.

Rattan Scrap Basket with Broad Band Near the Base

Materials: 8 46-inch spokes of No. 5 rattan,
1 24-inch spoke of No. 5 rattan,
16 23-inch spokes of No. 5 rattan,
22 weavers of No. 3 rattan,
4 weavers of No. 3 green rattan,
A pair of scissors,
A knitting needle,
A knife.

The bottom of this basket is started as in the directions for the rattan and rush basket, except that in this one the bottom is much smaller, being only five and three-quarters inches in diameter. The spokes are then wet and turned up with a slight flare.

When six full length weavers have been used in under-and-over weaving, a row of triple twist is made and then two green weavers, stained according to the directions in Chapter XII, are started in double weave to make the band, which should be two inches wide and will take four weavers. A row of triple twist makes a finish on the upper edge of the band and the under-and-over weaving begins again, gradually flaring until when it measures five inches from the top of the band it is thirty-six and a half inches in circumference. The spokes are then bent in, and the weaver drawn tightly until an inch and a half has been woven from the turn, when it is bound off and a border is made as follows: After soaking the spokes till they are pliable, a small piece is cut from the right side of each near the weaving, as previously described.

This border is in three rows. In the first row each spoke is brought back of the next spoke and then out. In the second row each spoke is brought back of the two succeeding ones and then out. It must be remembered in this process that the back spoke of the pair, made by bringing the previous spoke through, is always the one to use. In the third row each end of a spoke is brought over two spokes and pushed down inside the basket just behind the next spoke.

Rattan Scrap Basket with Broad Band Near the Top

Materials: 8 46-inch spokes of No. 5 rattan,
1 24-inch spoke of No. 5 rattan,
16 23-inch spokes of No. 5 rattan,
26 weavers of No. 3 rattan,
3 weavers of No. 4 rattan,
4 weavers of No. 3 terra-cotta rattan,
A knife,
A knitting needle.

This basket is started in the same way as the others, by slitting the horizontal spokes and slipping the vertical ones through them, then inserting the extra spokes when the bottom is large enough to admit them. When the bottom is five and three-quarters inches in diameter the side spokes are wet and turned up and rows of under-and-over weaving are formed into a bowl shape, which reaches thirty-five inches in circumference at its widest point. The spokes are then gradually drawn in by tightening the weavers until where the band at the top begins (about nine and three-quarters inches from the bottom); the diameter is not over nine and a half inches. Before starting the band a row of triple twist in No. 4 rattan is made and then the colored weavers, stained according to directions in Chapter XII, are woven in double weaving into a band two inches wide. Another row of triple twist in No. 4 rattan finishes the band, and two weavers of No. 3 make a slightly flared edge in under-and-over weaving, which is bound off and completed with this border.

The spokes are soaked and cut as in the previous descriptions. There are two rows in this border, and, as the second row is rather complicated, the beginning of that row should be left quite loose and open until the row is finished; enabling the worker to fit in the last three or four spokes in the border accurately and easily. In the first row the spokes are each brought back of the two succeeding spokes and then out.

In the second row the end of each spoke is brought under two ends, then over two and then down.

Small Scrap Basket for Desk or Table

Materials:
- 10 26-inch spokes of No. 4 rattan,
- 1 14-inch spoke of No. 4 rattan,
- 9 or 10 weavers of No. 2 rattan,
- 2 weavers of No. 2 green rattan.

A small basket to stand on a desk or table and catch bits of thread or a letter, hastily torn up, is a convenience the housekeeper will appreciate. One that is quite decorative as well as useful is made as follows: A flat bottom, two and seven-eighths inches in diameter, is woven on ten and a half spokes twenty-six inches long. The spokes are wet until pliable and turned up with a flare. The under-and-over weaving continues up the sides for half an inch, and then a row of double weaving in green rattan makes a narrow band. The sides, still flaring, are woven in under-and-over weaving for two and a half inches more; then another row of double weaving in green is followed by four rows of double weaving in the natural colored rattan. A row of double weaving in green comes next, completing the ornamental band at the top, and after two rows of under-and-over weaving in the natural colored rattan have been woven the circumference of the basket should be twenty-two and three-quarters inches. The spokes are then thoroughly wet and drawn in by tightening the weaver. An inch more of under-and-over weaving draws the spokes in further with each row, following the model in the picture. The basket is then bound off and finished with this border. Each spoke is brought over the spoke on the right, under the next one, over the next, under the next and then out where it rests on the spoke ahead, and is cut off when the border is completed. In this, as in other elaborate borders, the first part is left loose and open until the last spokes have been woven in.

Small Scrap Basket with Straight Sides

Materials: 8 26-inch spokes of No. 4 rattan,
1 14-inch spoke of No. 4 rattan,
8 or 10 weavers of No. 2 rattan,
6 strands of raffia braided and colored.

Another scrap basket for a desk or table is woven on eight and a half twenty-six inch spokes. A flat bottom three and a half inches in diameter is first made; the spokes are then thoroughly wet and turned sharply upward with about half an inch of triple twist to begin the straight sides. Two and a half inches in under-and-over weaving continue the sides, then three rows of braided raffia (colored with terra-cotta stain—see Chapter XII) make an effective band, which is followed by another two and a half inches of under-and-over weaving in rattan and half an inch of triple twist to form the edge. The border is made in two rows. In the first row each spoke is brought back of the next one on the right and then out, and in the second row each end is brought back of the next two spokes on the right and out, where it is cut just long enough to lie against the spoke ahead.

Birds' Nests

CHAPTER X

BIRDS' NESTS

AT the Bird Market in Paris fascinating little nests are sold. They are woven on spokes of twigs with weavers of rush. Why should not American children, who are learning to know and love the birds, make these inviting houses and hang them in the branches of trees for the wrens and other bird neighbors to settle in? Of course they must be inconspicuous in material and finish, for no self-respecting and self-preserving bird would choose a gaily colored or decorated nest. So it will be wise to make use of all the natural materials we can find—rush and raffia and perhaps even willow twigs and grasses; and when we use rattan let us stain it with dull shades of brown, green or gray.

Green Rush Bird's Nest

Materials: 6 14-inch spokes of No. 3 rattan,
1 8-inch spoke of No. 3 rattan,
¼ weaver of No. 2 rattan,
Green rush,
1 strand of raffia,
A piece of wire 6 inches long about the size of No. 1 rattan,
A pair of pliers.

Flat rush in its natural color, dull green, is used in weaving this little nest which will be soft and comfortable and suggestive of meadows and quiet streams to the fortunate bird who finds it. It is begun in the same way as the first baskets, with two groups of spokes crossed in the centre. A weaver of rush is bound around the spokes twice, then another weaver is started and the nest is woven in pairing into a bowl shape which, at about two and a half inches from the centre, should be eleven inches in circumference. This is the widest point. A row of pairing in No. 2 rattan is next woven and then the doorway is made. A weaver of rush is started in under-and-over weaving and woven until it comes to the part of the nest which has been chosen for the front. Here it is doubled back around a spoke and woven from right to left until it comes to the second spoke to the right of the one it first doubled around. It is brought around this spoke, thus making the beginning of a doorway, having an unused spoke in the centre of it. The weaver then returns to the spoke it first doubled around, where it doubles back again; and this is repeated until the weaver has been brought around five times on each side of the doorway, the spokes being slightly drawn in each time, so as to make the wigwam shape shown in the picture. After the weaver has been brought around the spoke on the right of the doorway the fifth time, at the point where the under-and-over weaving began, a second weaver is started and the nest is finished in pairing. The more slender rushes are used near the top so that the spokes can be drawn in very closely. The spoke in the centre of the doorway is now cut close to the weaving at the bottom of the opening and after it has been wet until pliable it is bent and pushed up between the weaving of the upper part of the nest, beside its own upper end. A strand of raffia is wound several times around the ends of the spokes at the top and tied in a loop by which the nest may be suspended from a convenient branch. A nest like this is often hung in an aviary or cage and when it is to be used in this way a hook made as follows is inserted at the back of the nest. A piece of wire, about as thick as No. 1 rattan and six inches long, is bent into a shape like

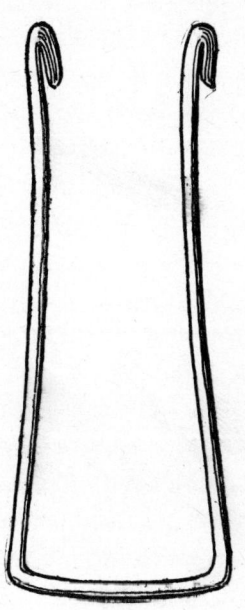

Fig. 23

Fig. 23, and pushed in between the weaving at the back of the nest (from the outside) at about an inch and a half from the centre. It passes up behind four or five rows of weaving, the ends coming out just below the row of pairing in No. 2 rattan, where they are bent down to form a hook or pair of hooks.

Rattan Bird's Nest with Raffia Top

Materials: 8 20-inch spokes of No. 4 rattan,
 1 11-inch spoke of No. 4 rattan,
 4½ weavers of No. 2 rattan,
 1 strand of raffia,
 A knitting needle.

In starting this nest the spokes are crossed and bound as for a basket, except that from the very centre they are turned up in a bowl shape. It is woven in under-and-over weaving in No. 2 rattan until at three inches and a quarter from the centre it measures fourteen inches in circumference. Here a doorway is made as already described, except that two spokes, instead of one, are left unused in the middle of the doorway, making a larger opening, and the weavers, which are doubled back to form the doorway, turn thirteen times. As in the green rush nest the spokes are drawn in by tightening the weavers from the bottom of the

BIRDS' NESTS

The large nests in the foreground are of rattan. The small one on the right is of brown rush, the nest above it is of raffia woven on rattan spokes, and the one on the left is made of a gourd covered with a netting of raffia

doorway up to the top of the nest, where they come together like the poles of a wigwam. At about an inch and three-quarters from the top of the doorway the spokes come so close together that it is almost impossible to use a rattan weaver, so a strand of raffia is started in under-and-over weaving and woven for an inch and a quarter into a soft roof. The two unused spokes in the doorway are next cut close to the weaving, at the top and bottom of the opening, and a rattan ring, by which to hang the nest, is made as follows: Half a weaver of No. 2 rattan, which has been wet until perfectly pliable, is passed, from the outside, through the top of the nest just under the last row of rattan, and out on the opposite side. Here it is tied through the other end of the weaver into a ring three and three-quarters inches in diameter. The ends are twisted around and around this foundation ring, as described on page 39, three or four times, passing through the top of the nest in each circuit until, when the ring is thick enough, each end is brought under one spoke, over another, and then cut short and pressed inside the nest. It should be finished with a coat of creosote shingle stain in gray, dull green or brown.

Raffia and Rattan Bird's Nest

Materials: 8 14-inch spokes of No. 3 rattan,
1 8-inch spoke of No. 3 rattan,
1½ weavers of No. 2 rattan,
A bunch of raffia,
A tapestry needle, No. 19.

A nest which has the scent of the woods about it is woven of raffia and rattan. It is soft, light and firm, and as pretty as can be. Two groups of spokes, one of four and the other of four and a half, are crossed in the centre, bound three times with a strand of raffia and woven in under-and-over weaving into a bottom an inch and a half in diameter. Here another weaver is added and an inch of pairing woven, forming the bottom into a bowl shape with sides rounding up from the very centre. A row of pairing in No. 2 rattan is next woven, to hold the slippery raffia firmly in place. This is followed by five-eighths of an inch of raffia in pairing, the sides still being flared. Then two rows of pairing in No. 2 rattan are woven, drawing the spokes in very slightly. At this point, the widest, the nest should measure eleven inches in circumference. A row of under-and-over weaving is started, and at the place chosen for the doorway the weaver is doubled back on two spokes, one on either side of a spoke in the centre of the doorway, and a doorway is formed as in previous descriptions. The weavers are doubled around the spokes which form the sides of the doorway eight times. Two rows of pairing in No. 2 rattan are then woven all the way around, forming a firm top for the doorway where they cross it. The spokes are drawn in closer and closer with rows of pairing in raffia until, when an inch and a half has been woven, they meet at the top. They are left uneven lengths and bound around several times with a strand of raffia, threaded through a tapestry needle. A loop made of two strands of raffia, five and a half inches long, is then covered close with button-hole stitch in raffia, which makes it neat and strong enough to hold the picturesque little nest securely in place. The spoke in the centre of the doorway should be cut, at the lower part of the opening just above the weaving, and, after it has been wet until quite pliable, bent and pressed up beside the upper part of the same spoke between the weaving. A hook, like the one previously described, may be added if the nest is to be hung in a cage or aviary.

Rattan Bird's Nest with Twisted Handle

Materials: NEST—6 24-inch spokes of No. 4 rattan,
1 13-inch spoke of No. 4 rattan,
6½ weavers of No. 2 rattan,
HANDLE—1 15-inch spoke of No. 4 rattan,
1 weaver of No. 2 rattan,
A knitting needle.

This nest is larger than any of the others described in this chapter, and is not closed at the top in the wigwam shape. The bottom is more like a basket than those of the other nests, being woven, in under-and-over weaving, into a flat centre two inches in diameter. The spokes are then wet until quite pliable and turned upward with a very slight flare for about five-eighths of an inch, where they are flared much more, and the weaver is left quite loose until about two inches more have been woven, when the circumference should measure seventeen inches. From here the spokes are gradually drawn in, with a tightened weaver, and at about three inches from the bottom the doorway is formed. The weavers on either side of the doorway are doubled back eleven times, drawing them in slightly each time. Two inches and a quarter of weaving are made above the doorway and then, when the opening at the top is about two inches in diameter, it is bound off and finished with this border. The spokes having been wet until they are thoroughly pliable, each is brought back of the next one on the right, in front of the next and then down inside the nest. A handle is made in this way. The ends of the fifteen-inch spoke are inserted, one on either side of the nest, at about three and three-quarters inches from the top, beside a spoke. On this foundation a weaver of No. 2 rattan is wound, as described on page 53, making a twisted handle. The nest is then colored a wood-brown with creosote shingle stain.

Bird's Nest Made of a Gourd Covered with Knotted Raffia

Materials: A round gourd about 11½ inches in circumference,
A bunch of raffia,
A flat stick about 1 inch wide and ½ a yard long,
A tapestry needle, No. 19,
A pair of scissors.

The negroes in the South often nail gourds to poles and trees for the birds to nest in. Borrowing their idea, why not inclose a gourd in knotted raffia, suspending it by a soft handle of braided raffia, which can be so twisted as to hold the nest at the angle best calculated to suit its tenants? If you are so fortunate as to have a gourd vine growing in your garden the most important part of this nest will be easily obtained. If not, however, you can probably buy one for a few cents at a shop where natural curiosities are sold. The one in the picture came from such a shop, but then it had a long, twisted handle. This was cut short, and then fourteen strands of raffia were knotted around a stick, as described in the directions for a knotted work bag in Chapter II. When five rows of knotting had been completed, the work was slipped off and finished. A strand of raffia was next passed through the lowest meshes and drawn up tight. The ends of the strands were cut close at the bottom, and after two small holes had been made, half an inch apart, through the soft gourd at about quarter of an inch from the edge and exactly opposite the stump of the handle, the knotted bag was drawn up over the gourd and fastened by passing a mesh of the first row over the handle. It was further secured by threading a strand of raffia through the loops at the top of the knotted bag, drawing it up close around the opening at the top and passing the ends through the holes in the front of the gourd, where they were firmly tied.

A braided handle was made as follows: Six strands of raffia, doubled in the centre, were braided until the braid (each strand of which was made of four strands of raffia) was long enough to reach up (from the outside) through the hole where the handle was cut off, out over the edge of the gourd and back to the starting point, where it was passed through the loop in the end of the braid. Here it was braided in two plaits, three inches and a quarter long, which were brought over in a double handle to the edge of the gourd, where the strands were all united again in one braid. This was brought down for about an inch inside of the gourd, where it was tied fast to the first braid and the ends cut short, completing this curious little nest.

Oval Baskets

CHAPTER XI

OVAL BASKETS

THE chief difference between the round baskets we have been weaving and these oval ones is, of course, in the centre (a notable exception being the Japanese basket on page 133, which slopes gracefully up from the sides to the ends), so that the aim in this chapter is to give the worker as great a variety in the pattern and form of these centres as possible.

English Oval Basket

Materials: BASKET—6 6-inch spokes of No. 3 rattan,
            1 3-inch spoke of No. 3 rattan,
            64 14-inch spokes of No. 3 rattan,
            6 weavers of No. 2 rattan,
            Brown rush.
HANDLE—2 35-inch pieces of No. 4 rattan,
            Brown rush,
            A knitting needle.

The six six-inch spokes are separated into pairs and laid on a table horizontally, leaving an inch between each pair. The short spoke, three inches long (which is cut pointed at each end), is laid vertically under the middle pair and in the centre of it, with its ends over the other two pairs. A weaver is then started, at the left of the short spoke, with its short end extending about five inches below the lowest pair; it is woven under the lowest pair of spokes, over the middle and under the upper pair. Another weaver is started at the left of the first, leaving a short end five inches below the lowest pair of spokes, and this goes over the lowest, under the middle and over the upper pairs of spokes. A second pair of weavers is started in the same way at the right of the short spoke, only with their ends, five inches long, turning up instead of down. These short ends are used as spokes later on. The weavers at the right of the centre are woven across the pairs of spokes in under-and-over weaving, as the first two weavers were. The sides are then pressed closely in together, forming the centre of an oval bottom, which is held in the left hand while the right weaves. The inner weaver on the left is brought over the short ends of the weavers on the right, under the right end of the upper pair of spokes, over the middle pair and under the lowest. The outer weaver follows, but in reverse order. The pair of weavers on the right is treated in the same way and then the weaving is done by pairing, using the pairs of weavers alternately. When the bottom is about an inch and a half across, the pairs of spokes are separated, and the pairing continues until the bottom measures three by five and a half inches. The ends of the spokes are then thoroughly wet, and two of the fourteen-inch pieces of No. 3 rattan are inserted on either side of each spoke to form the side spokes. These spokes are

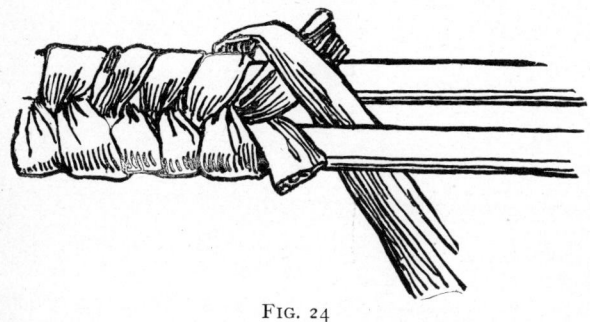

FIG. 24

turned up, flaring those on the ends of the basket more than the ones on the sides, and half an inch of triple twist is woven in No. 2 rattan. Two thirty-five-inch spokes of No. 4 rattan are inserted here to form a foundation handle. The ends of these spokes should be placed in the centre of a group of spokes and, on the other side of the basket, in the centre of a group that is exactly opposite. Two pieces of brown rush are next started, where the triple twist stopped, and are woven in pairing for an inch and a quarter, remembering always to flare the end spokes and press those on the sides in. The groups of spokes are now divided into pairs, and three-quarters of an inch of pairing in No. 2 rattan, with the following border, completes the basket. In the first row each pair of spokes is brought under the next pair on the right, over the next, under the next and outside the basket. In the second row each pair of ends is brought under the next pair on the right, over the next and down, leaving the first part of the row quite loose until the last part is finished, when the spokes are cut short. The handle is covered with rush in the way described on page 87. In joining new pieces of rush the ends are crossed on the uncovered spokes—see Fig. 24—and covered by the rush as the work proceeds.

Fayal Oval Basket

Materials: 6 5-inch spokes of No. 4 rattan,
4 7-inch spokes of No. 4 rattan,
1 4-inch spoke of No. 4 rattan,
84 12-inch pieces of No. 2 rattan,
2 weavers of No. 2 rattan.

The six five-inch spokes are slit for about three-quarters of an inch in the middle of each. The four seven-inch spokes, with the one four-inch spoke between them, are slipped through the six slit ones, leaving about half an inch between each of the six. The group of four and a half spokes are held in a vertical position, while the six run horizontally. A weaver is started, back of the vertical spokes and lying along the uppermost horizontal spoke, with its end toward the right. It is brought around in front of the vertical spokes (above the upper horizontal one), then back and down diagonally to the left, coming out below the upper horizontal spoke. Here it is brought around in front of the vertical group, back and up diagonally to the left of the vertical spokes and above the first horizontal one. It is then brought diagonally down, in front of the vertical spokes, to the right of them and just above the second horizontal spoke. Next it crosses diagonally down and back of the vertical spokes, to the left of them and below the second horizontal spoke, where it is brought over the vertical ones, back and up diagonally to the left of the vertical spokes, and just above the second horizontal one—see Fig. 25. The same process binds the other four horizontal spokes; making an ornamental cross effect over each one, on the inside of the basket—see Fig. 26. After all six horizontal spokes have been bound the spokes are separated and the weaving begins. When a bottom, four and a half by six and three-quarters inches, has been woven two pieces of No. 2

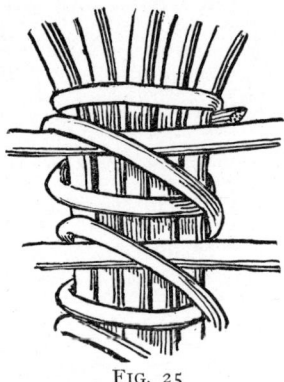

Fig. 25

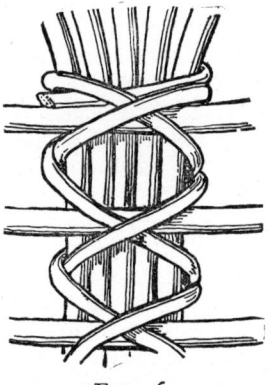

Fig. 26

rattan, twelve inches long, are inserted on either side of each spoke to form the side spokes. They are wet until quite pliable, and then each group of spokes is brought over the one on the right of it, under the next group, over the next, then under the next and out, drawing the groups in (except the first two or three, which are left loose until the last groups have been woven in), so that they will form close sides about two inches high. The ends of the groups are woven into a base as follows: The basket is turned upside down, and the ends of each group are brought over the next group on the left and pressed down inside the base, where they are afterward cut short.

Japanese Oval Bàsket

Materials: BASKET—4 28-inch spokes of No. 4 rattan,
1 15-inch spoke of No. 4 rattan,
6 26-inch spokes of No. 4 rattan,
12 weavers of No. 2 rattan.
HANDLE AND BASE—9 34-inch pieces of No. 2 rattan,
21 5-inch pieces of No. 3 rattan,
A knitting needle.

One of the most attractive oval baskets is copied from a Japanese model as follows: The six twenty-six inch spokes of No. 4 rattan are laid on a table horizontally; across these vertically the four twenty-eight inch spokes, with the fifteen-inch spoke between them, are placed. The end of a very-pliable weaver is laid along the top of the uppermost horizontal spoke back of the vertical spokes with its tip toward the right. The weaver is then brought forward around the vertical spokes, down back of the upper horizontal spoke, then forward around the vertical spokes three times, down back of the second horizontal spoke on the right, over the vertical spokes (between the second and third horizontal spoke) three times. It is then brought back of the third horizontal spoke on the right, up and around the vertical spokes three times, and so on, until all of the horizontal spokes have been bound to the vertical ones in exactly the same way. After the weaver has passed down and back of the sixth horizontal spoke and around the vertical group three times, it is brought across to the left of the sixth horizontal spoke, where the under-and-over weaving begins. Another centre which, though more elaborate, has been found rather more satisfactory, is woven in this way.

Six twenty-six and four and a half twenty-eight inch spokes are used—the same number of spokes with which the first centre was started. The group of twenty-eight-inch spokes are held by the left hand, in a vertical position, and at an inch above the centre the first horizontal spoke is laid back of the vertical ones. Along this spoke and back of the vertical spokes, with its end toward the right, a weaver is started. It is brought around in front of the vertical group, down back of the right side of the first horizontal spoke, in front of the vertical group, up and back of the left side of the first horizontal spoke, and over the vertical group above the first binding (see Fig. 27). It is then brought down, back of the right side of the first horizontal spoke, across the vertical group to the left side of the second horizontal spoke, which is laid back of the vertical group at about half an inch below the first one. The weaver goes down back of this second horizontal spoke, in front of the vertical group, up back of the right side of the second horizontal spoke, over the vertical group and down back of the left side of the second horizontal spoke. A third horizontal spoke is then laid back of the vertical group, at half an inch below the second one. The weaver crosses in front of the vertical group, down and back of the third horizontal spoke on the right, then over the vertical group, up back of the third horizontal spoke on the left, across the vertical group and down back of

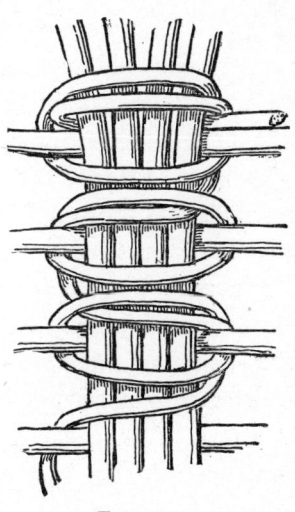

FIG. 27

the right side of the third horizontal spoke. A fourth horizontal spoke is laid back of the vertical group, half an inch below the third one, and bound in the same way as the others were. The same process also binds the fifth and sixth horizontal spokes to the vertical group. After the weaver has been brought down back of the left side of the sixth horizontal spoke for the second time, it crosses in front of the vertical group to the right side of the sixth horizontal spoke, where the under-and-over weaving is begun.

The bottom is woven two and a half inches wide by four inches long. The spokes are then wet until pliable, and bent sharply upward, flaring the spokes at the ends more than those at the sides of the basket. The nine pieces of No. 2 rattan, which are to form the handle, are inserted, five on one side and four on the other, of a spoke in the middle of one side of the basket, and the handle is made according to the directions for a braided handle on page 56. When the sides of the basket are about three and a quarter inches high the ends, which are to slope upward gradually, are woven in this way. When the weaver comes to the spoke at the left of the handle, it is doubled back and woven from right to left, all the way to the spoke at the right of the handle on the opposite side of the basket. Here it doubles around the spoke and returns, to be brought around the first spoke again and woven from right to left. On its second return it doubles on the spoke at the left of the one it started from, is brought around this twice in the same way, going to the second spoke at the right of the handle on the opposite side. It then

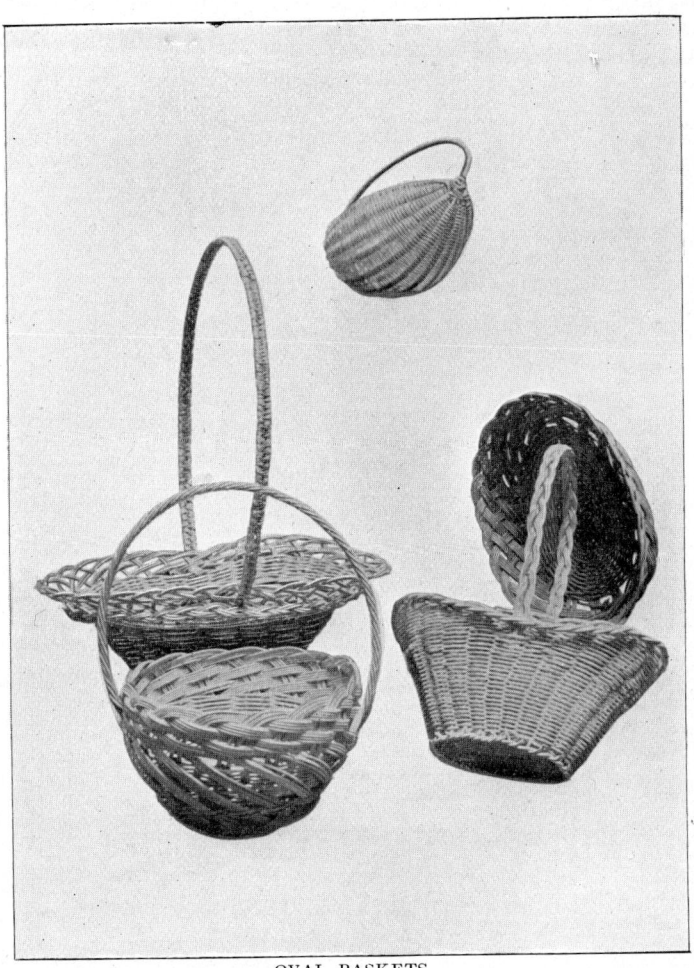

OVAL BASKETS

At the left of the foreground the Fayal basket with a handle is shown. Beside it is the Japanese basket, and back of that the ornamental centre of the other Fayal basket just shows. Above is the melon basket, and on the left the English model of brown rush and rattan

goes around the third spoke to the left of the starting point and the third to the right of the opposite handle twice, then around the fourth on each side, and so on, till the centre of the end of the basket is reached, when the end of the weaver is cut short and pressed down beside a spoke, and the other sloping end of the basket is woven in the same way. The border is made as follows: In the first row each spoke is brought back of the next spoke on the right and then out. In the second row, each end is brought over the next end and down, and in the third row each end is brought over the next twist on the right and down just in front of the next end. On the same principle as the Rope Border, the end next to be used is always the back one of the pair just made by bringing an end through. The base is made of the twenty-one five-inch pieces of No. 3 rattan, which are inserted (as the basket is held bottom upward) one on the left of each spoke, where the sides were turned up. There are two rows. In the first row each piece is brought over the next piece on the right and pressed down inside the base. In the second row each end is brought over the one on the right, and pressed down inside, making a roll like the Rope Border on page 39.

Fayal Oval Basket with Handle

Materials: BASKET—8 10-inch spokes of No. 4 rattan,
1 6-inch spoke of No. 4 rattan,
68 44-inch pieces of No. 2 rattan,
4 weavers of No. 2 rattan,
HANDLE—1 22-inch spoke of No. 6 rattan,
1 weaver of No. 2 rattan.

This model was copied from one of the sturdy Fayal baskets that the masters of sailing vessels used to bring home to our grandmothers in the good old times. In such baskets new laid eggs, fruit or a little pat of butter were carried to neighbors or sick friends.

The groups of four and four and a half spokes are crossed in the centre, just as the round centres are begun, but from the very beginning the oval should be formed by pressing the weavers close in on the sides and letting them go more easily on the ends. This method will make an excellent oval shape and one that is less complicated than any of the others. When about a weaver and a half has been used the forty-four inch pieces of No. 2 rattan, which serve as spokes, are inserted two on each side of a spoke. The bottom should be about six by four and a half inches when two weavers have been woven in. The spokes are then wet and turned up, keeping the oval shape; two more weavers are used in under-and-over weaving, the edge is bound off and the groups of spokes are woven into the following closed border. Each group is brought under the group on the right, over the next, under the next, over the next, under the next and outside of the basket, leaving the first two groups loose and open so as to allow the last ones to be woven in easily. Each group of ends is brought down on the outside of the basket, through a row of weaving, at about an inch and a half below the border, and just back of the third group of spokes from the one it last crossed. This holds the ends firmly in place. The basket is now turned upside down and two rows of pairing are woven to form the upper part of a base. The lower part is made by bringing each group of ends over the one on the left and down inside the base, where they are all cut off when the row is finished. The ends of a twenty-two inch spoke of No. 6 rattan are next inserted, below the border and down between a group of spokes, on each side of the basket to form a foundation for the handle which is the simple twisted one described on page 53.

Melon Shaped Basket

Materials: 1 21-inch spoke of No. 5 rattan,
1 23-inch spoke of No. 6 flat rattan,
8 10-inch spokes of No. 6 flat rattan,
20 or more lengths of narrow splint,
A piece of fine wire 5 or 6 inches long.

Although melon shaped baskets are graceful and attractive in form, the workman who undertakes to weave one will need a good stock of patience and skill, for they are among the most difficult baskets to make shapely and strong. On general principles it is well to have the spoke material as strong and unyielding as possible, while the weavers should be very pliable yet firm. Raffia is hard to manage as a weaver and rattan, unless it is unusually pliable, will break in making the sharp turns over the edge of the melon basket. The one in the picture is made of heavy round rattan for the edge, flat rattan for the spokes and handle, and narrow splint, such as is used by the Indians, for the weaver. The ten-inch spokes are first whittled to a gradual point at each end, a point from two and a half to three inches long. The ends of the twenty-three inch spoke of flat rattan are also pointed in the same way. The twenty-one inch spoke of No. 5 rattan is slit, for half an inch, in the centre and

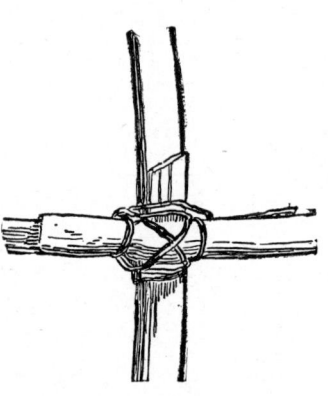

Fig. 28

whittled to a thin, flat point at each end. The piece of flat rattan which is to form the centre rib of the basket, as well as the handle, is passed through the slit in the twenty-one inch spoke (which is to form the rim of the basket) and its ends are brought together, between the two pointed ends of the twenty-one inch spoke, where they are bound securely with a piece of fine wire, see Fig. 28. In this basket there are two starting points, or centres, one at either side of the handle, and here the handle, rim and spokes are bound together. One way of doing this is as follows: The tips of eight spokes, four on each side of the central flat spoke or handle, are run up through the centre (where the handle and rim are crossed) and held in position by the left hand, while with the right hand a weaver is started back of the handle and lying along the rim spoke, with its end to the right. It is brought forward and diagonally down between the third and

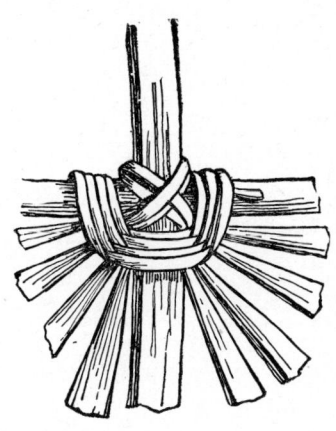

FIG. 29

fourth spoke from the handle, counting the rim spoke as one, see Fig. 29. The weaver is then brought back of five of the flat spokes, out and up diagonally to the right of the handle. Here it comes around again in the same way, binding the spokes securely in place. After the third time around, the weaver is brought over the three spokes on the right, under five and up around the three last spokes on the left, doubling over the rim on the left. In returning it is brought back of the three spokes on the left, in front of the five middle spokes and back of the three on the right, see Fig. 29. The weaver is bound around four times, in this way, and then the spokes are separated and the under-and-over weaving begins. Another pretty and simple centre is made as follows: The spokes, handle and rim are prepared as in the previous description, but the centre is started at the crossing of the rim and handle and the spokes are added as

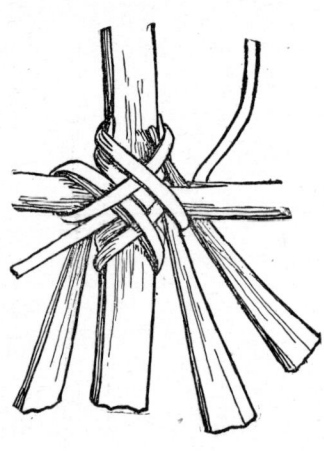

FIG. 30

OVAL BASKETS

the binding proceeds. An end of the weaver is started in front of the left side of the rim spoke and brought up and in front to the right of the upper part of the handle, back of the handle and diagonally down in front to the lower edge of the right side of the rim spoke. It goes up back of this spoke and diagonally down in front to the left of the lower part of the handle, where it is brought back and up from the right of the lower handle diagonally to the upper edge of the rim on the left. Here it goes around the rim spoke, and up diagonally to the starting point. One of the sharp pointed spokes is then inserted on either side of the handle, and the next time around the weaver is brought so as to bind the end of each spoke close to the handle. Then it passes around the rim spoke and the first spoke on the right, down and around the lower part of the handle as before, and up to the left, where it binds the left side of the rim spoke to the first spoke on the left, see Fig. 30. A spoke on either side of the handle is added each time and each time the ends of the spokes just added are bound in at the upper part of the handle. The spoke just added on the right is bound in with the rim spoke on the right by the weaver, which passes diagonally down below the rim and between the spoke just inserted and the previous one; up and back of the rim spoke, down diagonally, around the lower part of the handle and up diagonally, binding the spoke just added on the left to the left side of the rim spoke, as the one on the right was bound. When all the spokes have been secured in this way the weaving begins. An inch or two of under-and-over weaving is made, and then the spokes are brought up on each side of the opposite end of the handle, to start the other centre. The point of each spoke is pushed up through the slit part of the round spoke, where the handle was run through it. Here the binding process is repeated and, when an inch or two has been woven in under-and-over weaving, the weaving on the opposite side is begun again and woven to the middle of the basket, where it is met by the weaving from the second centre. The handle is wound with splint in this way. The spokes at one end of the handle are trimmed quite close, and a weaver is started near the handle and bound tightly around it, covering the foundation. If another weaver has to be joined to the first one, its end is pushed back under the rows of splint already wound. The end of the old weaver is laid along the uncovered handle and bound in as the winding proceeds. At the other end of the handle the tips of the flat spokes are trimmed close and covered neatly with the wound weaver, which is finally secured by weaving it under and over several spokes, cutting the end short inside the basket.

The Finishing Touch

Mordants.
① 3 oz. powdered alum — 1 qt of water.
② 1 Teaspoonful stannous chloride, 3/4 tea sp.
   cream tartar — 2 cups of water.

Brown (no mordant) logwood.
Red purple (soak raffia in alum)   solu
Blue   "   add few drops of ammonia to red purp
Black — Dip raffia in logwood, then take ou
   & add a small piece of copperas to Solut
   Put raffia back & boil 15 minutes —

Blue — Indigo (no mordant)
Green — Indigo & fustic (no mordant) Quercitron (C
Yellow Gr. — " & quercitron (alum mordant) —
Red — Cochineal (stannous chloride mordant)
     Boil cochineal & strain before putting in ra
Indian red — cochineal & fustic (alum mordan

  All raffia must be thoroughly soaked ei
in water or mordant, before dyeing & thorou
washed in soapy waters after dyeing —

Attioux — Purchase St, right hand side
  from Summer —
get sample sample bottles of logwood — fustic, Ind
Quercitron, cochineal —
buy alum stannous chloride, ortu crystals
copperal at drug store —

CHAPTER XII

THE FINISHING TOUCH.

In the process of making a basket there is no time when the individuality of the worker has a better opportunity to show itself than when he is putting the finishing touch. While the basket is still damp, all irregularities of shape which can be changed should be remedied. One side may be higher than the other, perhaps the border is not close to the weaving or the bottom may not be flat; now is the time to look for defects of form, before the rattan dries.

In soaking and weaving even the best rattan becomes somewhat rough, and little fibres protruding here and there do not look well. There are two ways of improving the surface: one is to singe the basket, which must be thoroughly dry, over a lamp; taking great care to hold it so that the fibres will be singed off without scorching the basket. Another and perhaps a better way is to sandpaper the rattan with No. 0 sandpaper until it is smooth. The basket is now prepared for the last process. This is either to finish the rattan in its natural color with a dull or polished surface, or to color it with stains or vegetable dyes.

Just a word as to aniline dyes. The Shah of Persia punishes with death the man who brings them into his kingdom, and we are tempted to exclaim with him "Off with his head!" when we hear of a person who, having seen the soft, beautiful coloring made with vegetable dyes, returns to the crude and quickly fading aniline colors. Laziness can be the only excuse, and even that is a poor one, for extracts of most of the vegetable dyes can be bought of dealers in dye woods in our principal cities, and the dyes are not hard to manage. Believing that only such colors as are found in natural basket materials should be used in basketry, but few dyes are mentioned in the following directions; but these suggestions will perhaps lead the worker to experiment further with vegetable dyes. It is a fascinating part of basketry, the coloring of materials, and yields large results for the time and trouble invested. Then, too, in experimenting with vegetable dyes the worker is naturally led out of doors and may discover dyes when he least expects them. For instance, one basket maker found in the purple iris a dye almost as deep as its own blossoms. The faded flowers are full of the purple liquid and, when they are rubbed on rattan, color it a beautiful shade which is quite as fast as most dyes.

Yellow from Fustic.—Before the rattan is dyed it should be soaked in a mordant or fixing bath. A solution of alum (three ounces of alum dissolved in a quart of water) is prepared and the rattan is laid in it over night. If the dye is to be extracted from fustic chips, the chips must be soaked over night in enough water to cover them and boiled next day in the same water, for fifteen or twenty minutes or just long enough to extract a bright yellow. A bit of rattan, which has been soaked in the alum bath, is dipped in from time to time to try the color. As soon as the rattan turns a bright yellow the dye should be taken off and strained, as longer boiling will turn it to duller olive shades. The extract of fustic will give surer results with less labor. It should be diluted with hot water. Cochineal added to fustic produces a dull red orange.

Brown from Logwood.—Logwood chips boiled in enough water to cover them, for fifteen or twenty minutes, yield a yellow brown. The rattan is simply soaked in the extract for several hours, or boiled in it, and then dried; no mordant being used.

Purple Shades from Logwood.—The alum mordant is used as previously described. The rattan is then dyed a soft purple by soaking it for a few hours, or boiling it, in the extract of logwood, obtained from the chips; or in the extract sold by dye houses, diluted to the right consistency with hot water. The addition of ammonia or baking soda will give a bluer purple.

Black from Logwood.—In the days when our grandmothers made their own ink every one knew how to obtain this dye. Boil the rattan in a decoction of fifty parts of logwood to ten of fustic, for half an hour. Remove the rattan and add four parts of copperas. Return the rattan and boil ten or fifteen minutes.

Orange from Annatto.—A bright orange is made from annatto in this way. A short time before it is required for use, it is dissolved by boiling it with a solution of carbonate of soda (washing soda) for twenty minutes. Mordant the rattan with stannous chloride (or tin crystals, which dissolve in a small quantity of water) and dye.

Orange from Quercitron.—The dyeing properties of quercitron are very like those of fustic, but with a mordant of stannous chloride its yellows are more orange than the fustic colors. Mordant the rattan with a solution of stannous chloride;

THE FINISHING TOUCH

and if the extract of quercitron is to be used, dilute it with boiling water and dye.

Scarlet from Cochineal.—Mordant the rattan with six parts of stannous chloride (crystals) to four parts of cream of tartar. Dye with cochineal (which has been boiled and strained) until the desired color is obtained.

The use of wood stains on rattan seems appropriate, for what is rattan but wood? Beautiful shades of green are obtained by adding a few drops of malachite green or green oak stain to different combinations of turpentine and linseed oil, or turpentine and varnish. These are so satisfactory that they take the place of green dyes which are more uncertain and more difficult to use on the rattan. People who like the natural color of rattan, but do not care for the dry, unfinished look of its surface will find either of the two following receipts useful. The polish, while not very shiny, acts like a varnish and strengthens and stiffens the rattan, making it slightly darker and yellower in tone. It is often used as a finish for scrap baskets, particularly those made of braided rush and rattan.

Polish.—Equal parts of turpentine and a varnish, known commercially as Light Oil Finish, are thoroughly mixed and applied to the basket inside and out with a stiff paint brush. If it is not possible to obtain the Light Oil Finish a common copal and turpentine varnish, rather dark, may be used, but this will require two parts of turpentine to one of the varnish. After the polish is dry any roughness may be removed with powdered pumice.

Pale Oil Finish.—Makes the rattan smooth and glossy and slightly darker than the natural color. Three parts of linseed oil and one part of turpentine are mixed thoroughly together and rubbed into the rattan with a soft cloth. This finish dries slowly, but if it is well rubbed into the rattan it will not take so long.

Deeper Oil Finish.—Two parts of turpentine, four parts of linseed oil and one part of cherry stain, mixed thoroughly and rubbed well into the rattan, will make a rather darker finish. This as well as the other oil finishes may be used to polish the rattan before it is woven into baskets.

Green Oil Finish.—A light yellow green — a green with life in it—is made with twelve parts of turpentine, nine parts of linseed oil and malachite green stain, added drop by drop until the right shade is secured. In using this, as other stains and dyes, it is wise to try the color on a bit of rattan before putting it on the basket.

Pale Green Finish.—A few drops of malachite green stain added to five parts of Light Oil Finish and twenty-one parts of turpentine will make a pale silvery green. The surface of the rattan will be left quite dry, there is so much turpentine in the mixture, but some people prefer this look.

Green Polish.—To equal parts of turpentine and Light Oil Finish a few drops of malachite green are added and after mixing thoroughly it is put on with a brush to the basket or separate weavers which are to be colored.

Pale Olive Green Polish.—Green oak stain is added drop by drop to equal parts of turpentine and Light Oil Finish until the right shade is obtained, by testing it on a piece of rattan. The mixture is then applied with a stiff paint brush to the basket or rattan which is to be stained.

Orange Stain.—There is a curious coloring matter, known as Dragon's Blood, which is imported from China and is used by violin makers to color their fine varnishes. It may be bought at any drug store, in sticks, and when ground in alcohol it yields a beautiful orange red. This makes an excellent stain with which to color separate weavers of rattan and raffia, braided or loose, to be used in weaving bands of color on the plain rattan baskets.

Dull Terra Cotta Stain.—To five parts of Light Oil Finish and twenty-one parts of turpentine a few drops of cherry stain are added, until a deep enough shade is obtained. This makes a color very like the terra cotta in Indian baskets, and in combination with black is very effective on baskets of natural colored rattan.

Terra Cotta Polish.—Is made by adding a few drops of cherry stain to one part of Light Oil Finish and two parts of turpentine.

Creosote Stain for Birds' Nests.—The creosote stain used for coloring shingles is an admirable finish for birds' nests. It acts as a preservative and is sanitary and clean, as well as beautiful to the eye. Any of the dull greens, yellows, browns or grays are appropriate for the purpose.

How to Cane Chairs

CHAPTER XIII

HOW TO CANE CHAIRS

SMALL, square frames of wood with holes bored in them, at intervals of about an inch, and having two or more round pegs to fit the holes, are sold by dealers in kindergarten supplies. These are excellent for the beginner to use, instead of a chair seat, while he is learning how to cane. The cane is sold at basket factories and is usually designated as coarse, medium, fine or fine fine. It comes in long twists, like the rattan, and is pulled out in the same way from the loop end. Two patterns of caning are given, a simple one on a frame and one that is more elaborate on a chair seat.

Simple Cross Pattern.

A square frame with 2 or 3 wooden pegs,
8 or 10 lengths of fine cane.

The frame, with its smooth side up, is held on the lap of the worker, with its upper edge resting on a table or chair at a convenient height. If, as is the case with the frame in the picture, there is an even number of holes across the top and bottom, say sixteen, the worker counts from the left side eight holes at the bottom, and eight at the top, from the left side. This finding the approximate centre must always be the first step. A length of cane, previously wet for a few minutes, is drawn up through the hole in the centre of the lower edge of the frame and down through the corresponding hole in the top edge, where an end about two and a half inches long is left and a peg put in to hold it. The long end of cane at the lower edge is now brought up through the next hole on the right, taking care not to twist it; here a peg is put in and the cane is brought down through the first hole on the right of the centre at the top, where the peg (taken from the previous hole) is put in to hold it in place. The cane is brought up through the next hole to the right and so on to the right edge. It should not be put through the hole next the edge, as that would bring it over the wood and at the same time cover the holes, two important things to be avoided. The cane should not be drawn absolutely taut, for when the finishing row of diagonal weaving is put in it tightens the work and if it is already strained the last weaving will be difficult. The ends are fastened off on the wrong side. Each is brought twice through the next loop, see Fig. 31, creasing the cane sharply so it will hold. Another length of cane is started at the left of the centre and brought through the holes from there to the left side of the frame, in the same way as on the right. The end, if it is long enough, should be left to work in on another row. The frame is now filled with vertical lines of cane. A row of horizon-

FIG. 31

tal lines is next put in, in the same way; starting from the centre and working out to the edge on the right and then out to the edge on the left. This covers the frame with a network of squares. Diagonal lines are then begun, starting from the lower left-hand corner and running a length of cane to the upper right-hand corner (the long ends left from the first rows may be used instead of starting new lengths of cane); the work being done as before, first to the right and then to the left, till the frame is filled with a set of these diagonal lines, being careful, however, not to run a line over the wood at the corners. In the fourth row the lines run diagonally, from the lower right-hand corner to the upper left-hand corner, but in this row the cane is woven; first under a cross then over a single cane, under a cross and over a single cane (see Fig. 32). Each succeeding line is woven in the same way, under the crosses and over the single canes. If there is a professional chair caner

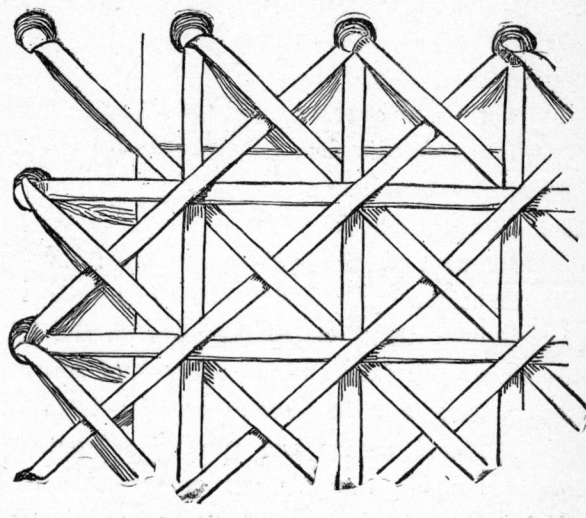

Fig. 32

in your neighborhood, it will help you to watch him at work, for caning is a process best learned by seeing it done.

Chair Seat with Octagonal Meshes

Materials:—A chair,
A bundle of fine cane,
A length of binding,
2 or 3 pegs.

CANING IN A FRAME AND ON A CHAIR

Two patterns of caning are illustrated in this plate. The simple cross pattern is shown in the frame on the wall, the more elaborate octagonal pattern on the chair

The more elaborate pattern with octagonal meshes, which is shown in the picture, is familiar to everyone. In fact, it is so generally used that if you are going to re-cane a chair you will very likely cut out a seat made in the same pattern. If so, cut it close to the wood all around and you will have a guide to help you in making the new seat. A foot-stool to sit on is a necessity, otherwise caning will be a back-breaking process. Seated on this stool the worker tips the front of the chair seat forward until it rests on his lap, and he is ready to begin. As in the caning previously described the centre must first be found, and the lines of cane run vertically across the seat. They should be left quite loose, or else at the sixth row of caning the work will be slow and difficult. One beginner made his first rows so tight that, when he came to the last row, he broke the frame of his chair trying to weave in the last lines of cane. The next set of canes are brought across the seat horizontally, these are followed by a vertical set of canes passing over the first vertical cancs, through the same holes. The fourth set of canes is woven horizontally across, first over one of the upper vertical canes, then under the lower vertical one, pulling the upper vertical cane in each group to the right and going over or under as the case may be. The chair seat is now filled with weaving which looks like Fig. 33. The next lines of cane run diagonally, from the lower left-hand corner to the upper right-hand corner of the seat. They go under the vertical pairs, and over the horizontal pairs to the right and above the vertical ones (see Fig. 34). The diagonal lines of cane which complete the pattern, go from the lower right-hand corner of the seat to the upper left-hand corner and pass always over the vertical groups and under the horizontal ones (see Fig. 34). In putting in the diagonal lines of cane it will often be found advisable to have two parallel lines begin or end in the same hole, especially at the corners. Look at some chair seat made in this pattern, and you will see an example. When this is done, the end of cane must either be brought through the loop next to it, before coming out through the same hole it went

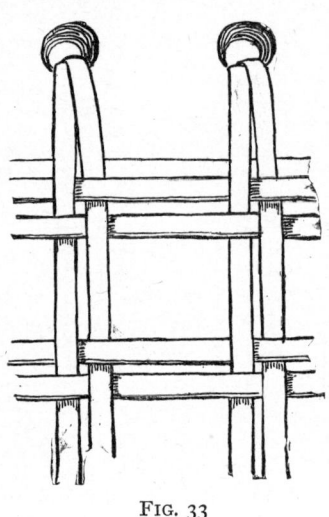

FIG. 33

in, or if it is a short end it is fastened off here and another started. In caning each chair there are small problems of this kind which the worker's common sense and sense of proportion will aid him to settle for himself.

When the last diagonal lines have been woven in the work is completed by covering the holes with a row of binding, as follows: A length of binding (cane which is wide enough to cover the holes in the edge, and is sold for the purpose) is brought up through a hole, at the right or left-hand upper corner of the seat, and laid along over the holes at the edge, where it is couched with a piece of fine rattan which is run up through every other hole, across the binding and back again. The process is repeated at every second hole on the right. When the circuit of the edge has been made, the binding is brought down through the hole where it started and there ended off.

FIG. 34

Some Indian Stitches

CHAPTER XIV

SOME INDIAN STITCHES

THERE is a charm in the names of such Indian materials as spruce-root, cedar-bark, yucca and Indian hemp, but even if they were obtainable, they would be useless to us without the Indian touch; so we will substitute more available materials, those we have become familiar with in the preceding chapters.

Rattan, both round and flat, in different sizes, may be used where a stiff, heavy material is needed, and raffia, rush, or split cane, where a more pliable one is required. Sweet-grass and the splints on which it is woven by the Eastern Indians and half-breeds may be bought, usually where the baskets are sold. In a previous chapter there is a description of the Indian arrangement of spokes. Where more than four spokes are to be used they are arranged according to the following diagram (Fig. 35).

Sometimes the weaver is of the plain sweet-grass, sometimes it is braided, and it is either woven in under-and-over weaving or pairing. If in under-and-over weaving, as there is an even number of spokes, the weaver at the beginning of the second row must pass under two spokes in order to have the work come out right. This must be done at the beginning of every new row. Pairing is not as often used by the Indians as the Indian pairing or twining. In twining the Indian twists her two weavers in the opposite way from ours (see Fig. 36), making a stitch which runs diagonally down from left to right. A half turn is given as in our method, but whereas in pairing the half turn is made as if one were turning a screw to fasten it, the motion in twining is that made when unscrewing. Usually but one spoke is inclosed by two of these twists, but sometimes, as in Fig. 37, the skip stitch, which incloses two spokes, is

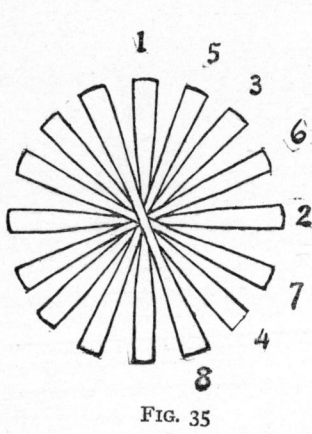

FIG. 35

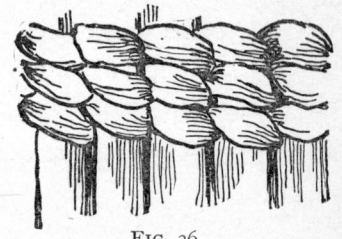

FIG. 36

introduced to form a pattern; and occasionally it is used for the body of the weaving (see Fig. 38).

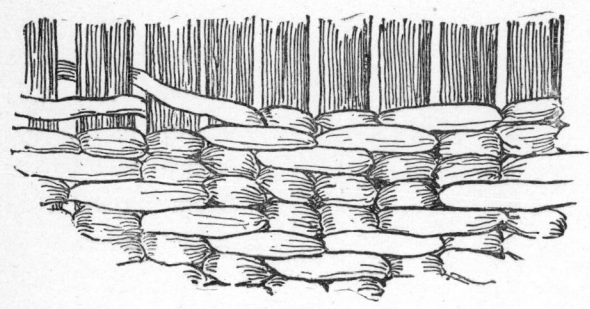

Fig. 37

Ornamental bands or patterns are often worked in stitches which pass between the two weavers, as in

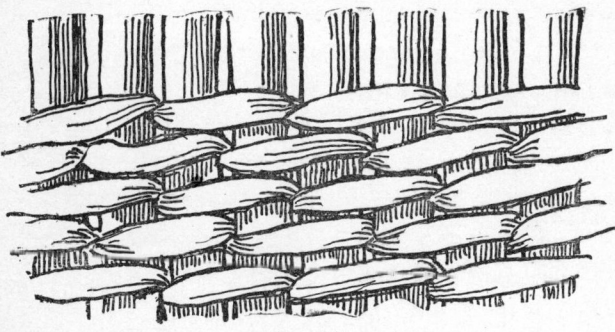

Fig. 38

aresene embroidery, showing only on the outside. These stitches give the effect of bands of pairing (see Fig. 39). Rows of twining are sometimes set far enough apart to produce an open work effect

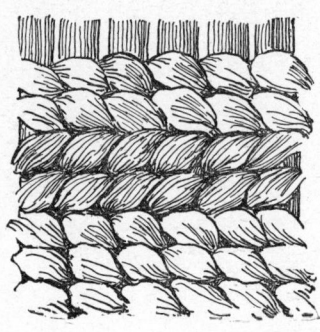

FIG. 39

(see Fig. 40). Again they form part of a diamond pattern like that shown in Fig. 41, which was copied from an Aleutian wallet of sea-grass. The spokes in the original are of coarse straw, but in working out the pattern raffia or rush may be used as spokes, and raffia for the weaver. The lower part of the pattern is in open work twining; the upper is made by splitting each spoke and joining the right half of each one with the left half of the spoke at the right of it, with twining. The succeeding rows are woven in the same way. Rows of twining are

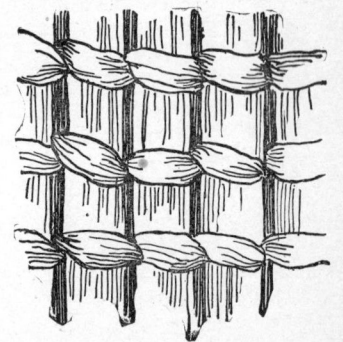

FIG. 40

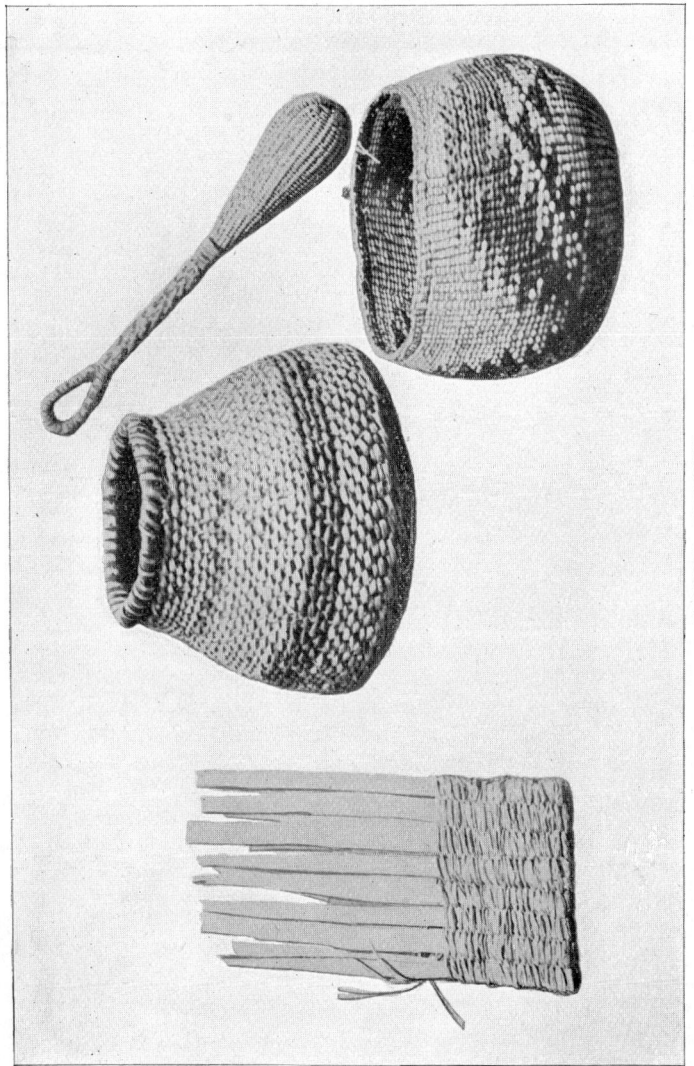

TWINED BASKETS

The basket in the centre is made with the twining which incloses two spokes in each stitch. The one at the right is of the simple twining. Above and on the right is a rattle made of raffia on rattan spokes. On the left the unfinished basket is of colored raffia on rush spokes

SOME INDIAN STITCHES

also used in a hexagonal pattern made by the Makah Indians (see Fig. 42). Bottles are often covered with this weave. The bottom is started with spokes radiating from the centre. Those in the original were of bast, but rush or raffia may be used. Every other spoke is brought diagonally to the right, crossing over the next one which is brought to the left. After crossing, the spokes are held in place by a row of twining. A charming wallet made by the Nez Percé Indians, from the bast of hemp, suggests a simple and attractive way of making a flat envelope shaped basket for photographs or postal cards. It may be woven on splints with sweet-grass, or even on flat rush with colored raffia. There should be as many spokes as, when laid side by side close together, will make the width desired. They should be cut twice and a half as long as the finished basket is

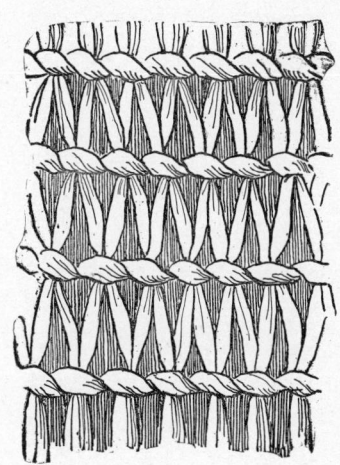

FIG. 41

to be. After wetting the spokes until they are quite pliable, a row of pairing is woven joining them together in the middle. The ends of the spokes are then brought up together, and by continuing the pairing around and around the

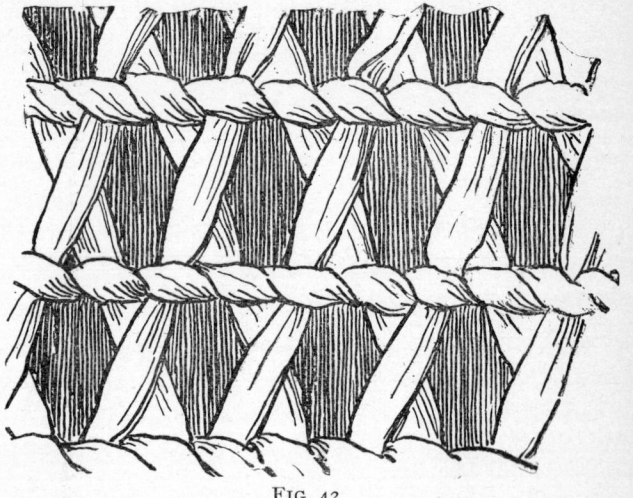

Fig. 42

basket is built up. The edge is finished as some of the sweet-grass baskets are. Every other spoke is cut short, while the alternate ones are left about three-quarters of an inch above the weaving. These are then thoroughly wet, and bent sharply down inside the basket over a piece of splint which is fitted around inside the rim of the basket with its ends overlapping. A second piece of splint covers the spokes on the inside and on the outside a rope of sweet-grass, or whatever the weaver may be, is laid around in the same way. A weaver is then started on the inside of the basket close to the edge and sewed over and over, passing between two spokes each time, and binding the splint on the inside and the rope on the outside close together, as it goes under and over them. A cover may be made just large enough to fit over the basket and finished in the same way. On such a basket, woven of pale green raffia, bands of raffia in the natural color are effective, or designs may be embroidered on it externally as already described.

The coiled baskets of the Apaches, Pai Utes, Navajo and Pimas are made of coiled osiers, or bundles of yucca whipped or wound with split osier or splints of pine. We can follow the stitch if not the rigidity and strength of these baskets by using single coils of No. 5 round rattan, or bundles made up of three or more strands of No. 2 rattan, coiled and wound with raffia. The rattan should be wet until pliable. It is then coiled into the smallest possible ring, and sewed over and over with a strand of raffia in a No. 19 tapestry needle. Beginning with the second coil, each time the raffia is wound around it is brought through the stitch just below it (see Fig. 43). Ornamental bands are sometimes added by laying a colored weaver along and catching it down with every third stitch (see

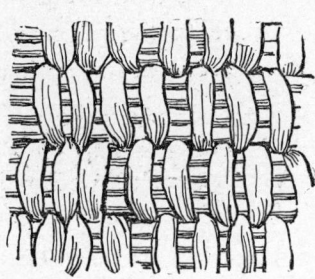

FIG. 43

Fig. 44). Another coiling stitch is made by bringing the weaver over the coil which has just been laid along and down under the coil below, locking into the stitch beneath that lower coil (see Fig. 45). A border which is often seen on coiled baskets, and which looks like braiding on a whip, is quite simple to make, much more so than one would think. A single weaver, preferably of splint, is passed under the sewing of the last coil, then drawn over it and backward. It is next brought under again, upward and forward, just in front of the point where it started.

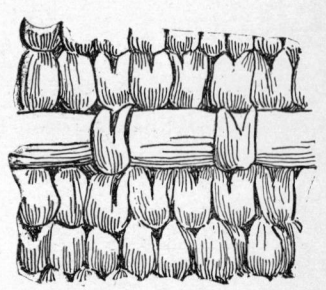

FIG. 44

In this way, by sewing first backward and then forward, as one

COILED BASKETS

SOME INDIAN STITCHES 177

would coil a kite string, the braided border is made with a single weaver. The bird-cage stitch of the Clallam and Makah Indians is sometimes woven with an open mesh, and sometimes close and fine. In copying the open-meshed weave shown in Fig. 46, No. 4 rattan may be used for the vertical spokes, No. 3 rattan for the horizontal coil and raffia for the weaver. The horizontal coil is laid back of the vertical spokes, and a single weaver of raffia binds the vertical spokes to the coil where they cross. The rows are about a quarter of an inch apart. In the close weave the spokes, horizontal coil and weaver are more uniform in size. No. 2 rattan

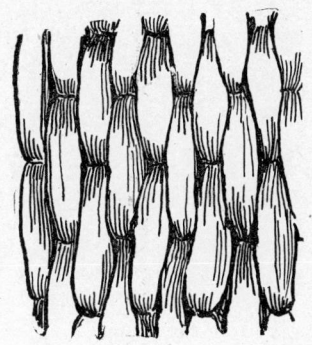

FIG. 45

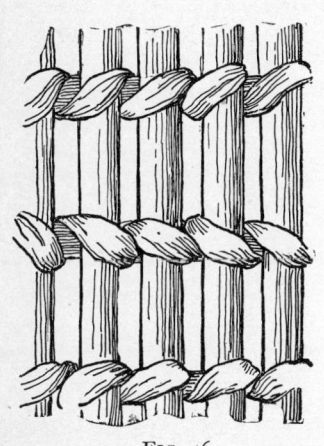

FIG. 46

may be used for the spokes and coil, and raffia for the weaver. The stitch is the same except that the rows are brought close together, and as the weaving progresses; the spokes, being quite pliable, bend forward in the direction the weaving takes; making an unusual and attractive surface (see Fig. 47).

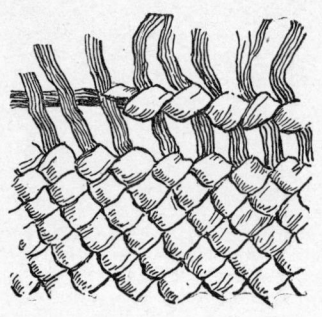

FIG. 47

What the Basket Means to the Indian

CHAPTER XV

WHAT THE BASKET MEANS TO THE INDIAN

BY NELTJE BLANCHAN

NOT through a written literature, not through music, architecture, sculpture or painting, as we understand the fine arts, has the North American Indian yet expressed the intellectual and spiritual aspirations of the race; but chiefly through the artistic handicrafts of the women.

While primitive man, of all races, waged war and hunted, of necessity, primitive woman was ever the constructive element in society, the home-maker, the conserver of industry and thrift, the manufacturer, through simple, homely processes, of the raw products of nature into useful and sometimes beautiful forms, the inventor of many crafts, the mother of the arts, the nurse of religion. To mention only one of her contributions to civilization, there is the textile handicraft, invented by aboriginal women the world around to meet the need for shelter, clothing, hats, cradles, fish and snaring nets, mats and baskets; and so thoroughly did they master the intricacies of weaving, that not a single new stitch has been added to the sum of primitive knowledge by the most skilled modern craftsmen. At the point where primitive women left off, civilized men, at a comparatively recent date, were able to take the work from their hands, apply machinery to it and convert the manufacture of textiles into one of the great staples of commerce for the world.

Through the same phases of development all races of mankind must pass, ethnology teaches us, and today our Indian woman is where Egyptian, Roman, Teuton, Frank and Briton women once were before their respective races attained civilization and culture. Like the Indian weaver in the West today, where civilization has not yet effaced her, these women of the ancient world were once the weavers for their people; references to their spinning, weaving, and basketry abound in early literatures, and examples of their similar work, still extant in museums, testify to the sisterhood of the human race. Into all these primitive home-made articles, beauty slowly found greater and greater expression in form, color and design; and it was often wrought out through materials so crude and difficult to manipulate as to make one wonder that effort to transform them was even attempted.

WICKER SCOOP—For gathering acorns and piñon nuts. BASKET BOWLS—In which acorns are boiled by the use of hot stones. A BOTTOMLESS BOWL—Placed over a hollow stone in which dried acorns are ground into meal. DINNER PLATES—Used by the Hupa Indians, California

(*Courtesy of The American Museum of Natural History, New York*)

Civilized man has yet to discover a use for the fretful porcupine, but Indian women have used its quills for centuries to embroider designs on household articles made of skin and bark. The Pimas and Apaches, living in the alkali desert of Arizona, utilize the "cat claws," the hard, stiff, black seed vessels of one of the few plants that can grow on their arid reservations, to weave the Greek key pattern, the mystical Swastika of India and Egyptian-like geometric, symbolic designs into their wonderful willow baskets. How much beauty would you and I attempt to put into our cooking utensils and articles of commonest household use with such a pitiful poverty of material?

With a more scientific appreciation of primitive woman's contribution to modern civilization must come a sympathetic interest in the handicrafts of our Indian woman, whose slow steps in upward progress we may even now behold her taking for her people. We may see the early industrial history of our own race repeating itself in the Western world.

Chief among the Indian's handicrafts is basketry: the most expressive vehicle of the tribe's individuality, the embodiment of its mythology and folk-lore, tradition, history, poetry, art and spiritual aspiration—in short, it is, to the Indian mind, all the arts in one. Moreover, it is his most useful handicraft, serving him from the cradle to the grave.

In a deftly woven bassinet, ornamented with shells, gay feathers or bits of bright cloth, such as any baby would enjoy, the Indian mother ties her papoose. Hanging the cradle from a sheltering tree while at work about the camp, or suspending it from her strong shoulders when she must wander afield, she allows the precious contents to interrupt her regular labors but little. Here, as in everything she makes, is the simple, perfect adaptation of the article to its uses which gives primitive handiwork everywhere so great an interest. It is only after we attain civilization that the meaningless multiplication of the unnecessaries begins.

When there is not a baby on her back the squaw has other burdens to carry—wood for the camp-fire, meat from the hunt, fish, grain, nuts, fruit and water; and, again, netted twine or woven basket serves every purpose. One of the most beautiful and expressive designs ever made by an untutored hand was wrought out in a large bag of netted yucca fibre deliberately manufactured as a wood carrier by a bronze savage girl in one of the out-of-the-way corners of the Southwest.

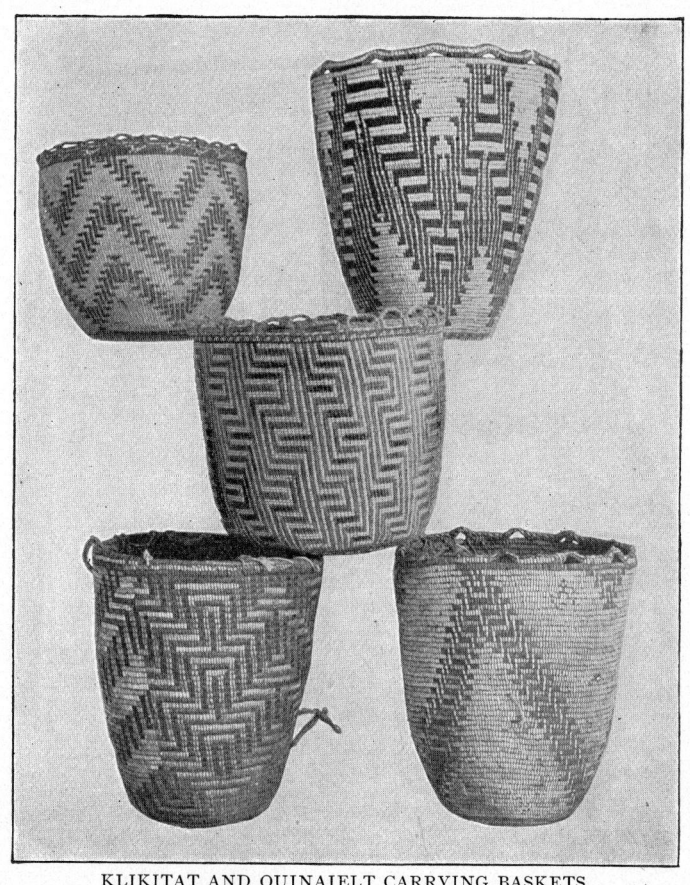

KLIKITAT AND QUINAIELT CARRYING BASKETS
(Oregon and Washington)
Designs represent mountains, streams, rippling waves and fertile valleys, where the plumed quail abounds
(*Courtesy of The American Museum of Natural History, New York*)

The shapes of carrying baskets differ widely. Originally both food and water were doubtless carried in hollow gourds enclosed in netted twine to give additional strength, and a stick slipped through the meshes made their transportation easy. But in due time the basket evolved from netting, and the cone-shaped carrying-baskets made by certain Western tribes today are of exceedingly beautiful workmanship. The finely woven decorations represent in symbolic, conventionalized form those familiar natural objects so dear to the Indian heart—mountains, lakes, streams, trees, sea waves or water fowl, for example—objects with which the particular tribe has closest association. These are the subjects such as ever stir the Indian artist's imagination.

How can water be carried in a basket? one may well ask. Strangely enough, the tribes living in the arid Southwest, where every drop of water is exceedingly precious, are the very ones which chiefly trust to basket water-carriers. No danger of the pitcher breaking at an Indian well. The Pai Utes, who make water-jars for their own use, and to barter for blankets with the Navajo, weave them of willow strippings and coat them with gum from the piñon pine. Many baskets made by various tribes are tightly enough woven, however, to hold water even without a gum coat. The bottom of the wicker water-bottle, made by the Havasupais in Cataract Cañon, Arizona, tapers to a point, which the Indian sticks into the ground to prevent the bottle from overturning. Handles of braided horsehair, which never break, confine the leather strap by which the squaw suspends the bottle from her head or her pony's saddle. Such bottles may be made to contain a pint or several gallons of water.

In the division of labor among primitive people, at least, women have always taken charge of the family larder. For collecting, preparing, cooking and serving food, basketry is still most important to the Indian. To gather the nuts under the piñon trees in the Rocky Mountain region, she fashions a spoon-shaped wicker scoop, whose bowl is also a coarse sieve through which the dirt is shaken. Huge storage baskets, representing tens of thousands of stitches, are often as tall as a man, as symmetrical as a Greek vase, and they are laboriously ornamented with symbolic designs which convey whole volumes of meaning to members of the tribe. The White Mountain Apaches, among others, make some wonderful household granaries. Into these great baskets the Indian housekeeper pours the nuts, acorns, fruit, maize,

ALASKAN WALLETS, CARRYING BASKETS, TREASURE BASKETS, PLATES AND ALEUTIAN EMBROIDERED WALLET

(Courtesy of The American Museum of Natural History, New York)

and other grains on her return from nature's market in the woods and fields.

Every Indian woman is her own miller. Going to a favorite rock, hollowed on its upper surface by much grinding, she places upon it a bowl-shaped but bottomless basket to confine the portion of grain being ground, as well as to prevent the wind from blowing away her meal. Through the hole in the bottom of the basket she works her stone pestle diligently until all the grain is ground fine. Even a prosaic basket like this one does not lack its appropriate, poetic symbols. A wicker winnower, to separate the grain from the chaff, is usually shaped like a large scallop shell, suggesting its probable derivation before the Indians were driven backward from the coast into the interior. A basket through which to sift the finer flour is a necessary utensil in every well-regulated Indian household. Today Chinese merchants still sift tea through basket trays.

The slightly hollowed basket plaque, which is one of the commonest and most widely distributed shapes, may be used as a meal tray in the pueblo home, or, heaped with propitiatory gifts to appease the wrath of an angry god, may adorn the village altar; again it is seen in use among the gamblers, who toss their dice upon it; at ceremonial dances of several tribes it is most important; the Navajo wedding feast cannot be eaten from any other dish; and when an Indian dies, members of the family reverently place food in basket plaques on the ground around his grave, that his spirit may refresh itself on its visits to earth. Because of the number of tribes using the plaque, and the great variety of uses to which it is put, no form of Indian basket shows more varied weaves and wider range of decorative design.

To interpret Indian symbols without the help of the squaw who worked them out of her own inner consciousness, to get at the thought of the individual weaver, taking into due consideration the mental idiosyncrasies of her tribe, as one must do before the decoration can be rightly understood, is an exceedingly difficult task which the enthusiast with a lively imagination would better leave to the scientific investigator. But no student of races, of the evolution of art, of folk-lore or of comparative religions, can afford to neglect the Indian basket. And the study cannot begin too soon, for basketry has either deteriorated sadly wherever the white people's civilization has penetrated, or it has totally disappeared. In one small collection of meal plaques alone are found three whose decorations tell of the creation of the world according to the legends of as many tribes; another plaque shows four streams flowing in regular, beautiful lines from a lake in the centre to the edge; a Hopi, yucca plaque, with unfinished end, reveals the age of the girl who wove it; a spider-web design wrought into another, is a prayer for rain to the spirit which presides over the gossamer clouds that bring it to the suffering people in the desert; a circle set with small stars represents the constellation Corona; a star which radiates toward every point of the compass may be read as a petition for favorable winds while the crops are growing, and yet, to another tribe, the same design may have a totally different significance. But every line on an Indian basket is eloquent with meaning if we could but interpret it—that is what makes the study of basketry so interesting to the collector and so important to the scientist. A pattern which looks like a flash of lightning to desert Indians, whose every thought is directed toward signs of rain, may mean a mountain stream to a tribe living among the Sierras, or, again, it may be intended to represent the incoming tide to Indians with homes near the sea. Still another grain plaque in this small collection, has for its border the rattlesnake's markings conventionalized, and it is a prayer laboriously and fervently expressed, asking for protection of the weaver's loved ones from the deadly rattler. This design, with various modifications which include the St. Andrew's cross, is especially common among the Indians in Northern California and Alaska, whose exquisite basketry, rich in symbolism, is not surpassed by any people in the world.

The acorn is a staple article of food among several tribes, but before it is fit for the human stomach it must first be boiled. How is the Indian, who has no pottery and who never saw an iron kettle, to boil her food? In California there are still to be seen a few squaws cooking in watertight baskets after the primitive method of their ancestors. Stones heated at a neighboring fire are tossed into the water until it is brought to the boiling point, and there it is kept by the addition of more hot stones until the acorns are cooked. Now all the bitterness is gone, and when dry again they are ready to be pounded into meal. The cooking basket of the Hoopa Valley Indians, for example, is a thing of beauty, with mountain peaks and flowing streams on its shapely sides. How repulsively ugly are the civilized cook's machine-made kitchen utensils compared with these hand-wrought vessels in which the Indian woman delights! With genuine artistic feeling she fashions her kettle from shreds of the red bud, mountain

APACHE GRAIN PLAQUES AND JARS (Arizona)

All made from the sisal willow strippings and the black seed vessels of a desert plant (*Martynia*) popularly known as the "Cat Claws"

(*Courtesy of The American Museum of Natural History, New York*)

grasses, colored with natural dyes, and stems of the maiden hair fern, the whole often representing weeks of work.

Ages before people had pottery to cook in they had basketry, which is, indeed, the oldest and the most universally practised handicraft known. Perhaps a hunter returned home hungry one day in the far away past, and his wife, anxious to hasten dinner for her impatient lord, coated her cooking basket with clay that she might set it directly over the fire without danger of burning. Imagine the woman's surprise and joy to find on removing it from the embers after dinner that she had a basket plus an earthenware pot! Thus directly from basketry was pottery evolved. One finds the same shaped vessels of clay as of wicker work among the Zuñi and other potters, and the same decorations in many instances on both. Moreover the Havasupai still use clay-lined basket-plaques to hold glowing wood embers and kernels of corn, which are kept dancing together by the dexterous cook until the corn is parched; meanwhile the clay hardens. Numbers of good cooking utensils are thus produced

Far to the North, where the cedar tree furnishes the wretched natives with practically every comfort they have, wooden cooking boxes, fashioned from its trunk, hold the water into which hot stones are tossed when fish or blubber is to be boiled. Clothing is woven from shredded cedar bark and mats for the weaver to sit upon. But even in this desolate, poor land, an earnest striving after some expression of beauty is seen. In the most remote islands in the Aleutian chain, the Indian woman, unrewarded by applause or hope of gain, weaves exquisitely fine, dainty treasure baskets, being impelled by impulses as natural as those of a bird whose weaving is scarcely less amazing. The longest, hardest journey is not too wearisome to deter a squaw from going to collect rare roots and grasses or dyeing material; a lifetime is not too long to perfect herself in the handicraft bequeathed to her as a tribal trust from former generations. When vegetable fibres seem inadequate for all the beauty she fain would express, the Poma weaver in California, adds rare feathers, wampum, alabone, and sometimes bits of silver, although the finished marvel is destined for the bonfire in the death dance ceremonial. One of these exceedingly fine Poma feather baskets, which is always as valuable as a pony, was recently sold to a museum for eight hundred dollars. "Datso-la-lee," a Washoe weaver whose skill is probably unrivaled in any land, has recently made an intricate basket that was sold for eighteen hundred

RARE POMA CEREMONIAL BASKET—Adorned with plumes of valley quail, wampum, shell, and feathers from the woodpecker's crown. MONO JAR. ALASKAN TREASURE BASKET—With snake rattles in cover. TWO ALASKAN CARRYING BASKETS. A SQUAW CAP—The design woven with stems of maiden-hair ferns. COOKING BASKET—Used by the Hupa Indians, California.

dollars to a private collector, and he possesses a masterpiece of art as truly as the connoisseur who invests thrice that sum in a piece of bronze or a painting. If the Indian woman reaped the profit of her toil, and not the frontier trader (who is a shark in far too many instances), there might be greater hope of preserving the native industries. As it is, they are perilously near becoming among the lost arts.

It would be interesting, if space permitted, to trace the influence of basketry on design in general, to show the necessary adoption of straight lines, geometric patterns, through the exigencies of wicker weaving. The Indian imitates what she sees about her; she is a silent, profound student of nature which she strives to copy; but in order that natural objects may come within the limitations of basketry—the principal medium of expression— every object has to be conventionalized, its form modified. The square-shouldered human figures, the angular beasts and birds depicted by the ancient Egyptians, are not very different from the Indian's attempts to reproduce these same forms on ceremonial dance baskets, granaries, and plaques, with uncompromising willow and grasses. Given more plastic material through which to express art ideals, the Indian potter evolved graceful scrolls and curves from the almost universal design known as the Greek meander or rectilinear fret and its variants, which have been favorite themes with our Indians from time immemorial.

The Indian is essentially artistic, not musical, like the African negro, and not literary, however masterful in the use of words in oratory. There is every reason to believe that our national art will receive new direction, a fresh impulse, from educated Indian Americans.

The poor Indian,

> "whose untutored mind
> Sees God in clouds and hears Him in the wind,"

has recorded a wealth of such spiritual visions in her baskets alone: scarcely one of them that does not contain a prayer. To how much of the handiwork of modern civilized women, tutored or untutored, could equal praise be given?

Date Due

| Jul 17 '51 | MAY 2 5 1983 | |